WORSHIPPING IN DARKNESS

REFLECTIONS ON *THE BOOK OF JOB*

TIM RASULOV

*iv*Pub

© 2010, 2019 by Tim Rasulov
Published by ivPub, Vancouver, WA

All rights reserved. No part of this publication may be reproduced in any form or by any means without the prior permission of the copyright owner, except for brief quotations for the purpose of review or comment.

Originally published in Russian as

Тимур Расулов
Поклонение во тьме
Размышления над книгой Иова
«Библия для всех»
Санкт-Петербург
2010

Unless otherwise noted, Scripture quotations are from the New American Standard Bible® (NASB), copyright © 1960, 1962, 1963, 1968, 1971, 1972, 1973, 1975, 1977, 1995 by The Lockman Foundation. Used by permission. www.Lockman.org

Scripture quotations noted NIV are from The Holy Bible, New International Version® NIV®, copyright © 1973, 1978, 1984, 2011 by Biblica, Inc.™ Used by permission. All rights reserved worldwide.

Translation from Russian by Evgeny Terekhin (www.russiantranslators.org)

English translation editing and proofreading by Michelle Morley

Cover design by Eugene Mishkin (www.youare.agency)

Typesetting by Andrey Raugas

Printed in the United States of America

ISBN: 978-0-578-52685-0

*Dedicated to missionaries
of The Evangelical Alliance Mission,
who brought the Light of Jesus Christ
to the darkness of my life:
Keith McCune, Carl Peklenk,
Herbert Gregg, Brent Preston,
their wives, and Christine Bordeaux.*

"The people who were sitting in darkness saw a great light, and those who were sitting in the land and shadow of death, upon them a light dawned."

(Matt. 4:16)

*Special thanks to Peter Gusev;
without you, this translated version
of my book would not exist.*

Contents

Foreword		7
1	The Great Drama. Prologue	11
2	Theological Difficulties	25
3	The Miserable Comforters	41
4	The Forgotten Character	63
5	Hope	81
6	The "Righteous" Rebellion	105
7	The Right of the Potter	125
8	The Right of the Potter (part 2)	145
9	The Meaning of Life	165
Epilogue		185

Foreword

Job captured my interest right away. No other book of the Old Testament was nearly as thought-provoking for me as the Book of Job; however, I remember being quite puzzled after the first reading. The ending left me with more questions than answers, and I was quite frankly disappointed. I even concluded that part of the book must have been lost, because the final chapters just didn't square with my expectations. I was hoping that in the end God would do something different for Job, perhaps give him some deeper, more specific answer. He could have been more compassionate to Job, or at least, given him some clarity! I thought to myself, "What's wrong with giving answers to the first godly man in the history of the world, considering everything he had to suffer?" God's way of dealing with him seemed more like muscle flexing and a vague threat, not a way to comfort someone. It seemed like some inscrutable demonstration of superiority, which was the last thing I would expect from a merciful heavenly Father.

    I found myself constantly thinking about Job. I had a feeling that this book of the Bible, which is probably the oldest in all of Scripture, contained answers to some of the most pressing questions about our relationships with God. What happened to Job shook me to the core of my being. My mind started racing back and forth as I attempted to find some logical explanation which would fit my then small-minded theology. What was happening to me then was very much like Abraham's tiptoeing alongside God as the Almighty was on His way to punish Sodom and Gomorrah (Gen. 18:20–33). The one who would become the forefather of a great nation challenged God with questions which curiously combined faith and doubt. He had to make sure that the One he put his trust in was in fact trustworthy. Knowing this righteous man's need, God was patient in answering his questions. Yet there comes a time when the Lord stops satisfying our curiosity. He intentionally leaves some space for our faith and trust to grow; unanswered questions are often the best soil for our faith to flourish in. I can very much relate to this in my own life. Sooner or later I was up against the wall of the "mysterious," but before I got there, the book provided me with some answers to the most important questions. For quite some time, I refused to accept certain things that surfaced during my study of the book. I kept questioning as though no explanation was to be found. But the truth is—it was there all along; I just didn't want to accept it. Sound familiar? Finally, I concluded that this study could last indefinitely, and I needed to face the facts which could only be accepted by faith. It was not a question of finding a logical solution; it was a question of humility and faith. This realization marked the beginning of my long journey through the pages of this surprising book of the Bible.

What you are about to read came out of years of study. As a Christian counselor, I often go to Job in my practice and this book has been written from a counseling perspective. This is not a Biblical commentary, but rather a general analysis emphasizing key themes and application. I hope to demonstrate that the Book of Job touches upon a wide range of themes, such as worship, the meaning of life, hope, enduring suffering, and understanding true compassion. It is through this message that the Church was inoculated against some of the most harmful heresies long before they appeared. And finally, this work is an attempt to inspire and equip the Church of Christ to serve God well. To Him alone be the glory in all things!

August 10, 2010.
Samara, Russia

1
THE GREAT DRAMA

PROLOGUE

There are at least three distinctive features of the Book of Job which must be accounted for in the course of interpretation. Unlike Romans, Job does not present God's truths in a continuous stream of impeccably consistent Biblical doctrines. One has to pull together the scattered pieces of the "mosaic" from various parts of the book. Middle-Eastern poetry, the Book of Job in particular (except for the three final chapters), is very different from Western poetry, especially its contemporary forms. The Western style is more like a soldier marching from point A to point B in measured steps. Everything is logical and clear. In Eastern style, may the reader forgive me, you have more of a drunkard meandering from point A to point B in mind-boggling zigzags, circles and dashes. One moment he is leaning against the wall, next he's hugging a tree, then he's taking a few steps forward and a few steps back in order to keep his balance. He's moving on to his goal, albeit constantly clinging to something and never traveling in a straight line. Take Psalms, for example. First of all, determining the structure of a Psalm is an ordeal. The structure is there, but those unfamiliar with chiastic structures will sweat before they find the pattern. There is no preacher out there who wouldn't wish that psalmists had been more Western in their thinking. But here we are dealing with the East, and we have to take stylistic differences into consideration.

Secondly, each character's monologue in and of itself will usually have one or two key ideas expressed in a purely poetic form, with repetitions and gradual unfolding throughout the narrative. There may also be smaller ideas attached to them, coming in bits and pieces like falling stars, burning brightly and not to be repeated again. Yet these smaller ideas may have the same or even greater theological import than their repeated counterparts (19:25). In this treasure trove of God's revelation we see more than meets the eye, just like in any other treasury of the Scriptures. The speeches of the main characters are replete with high-flown metaphors and comparisons, which at times make it hard to keep up with their theological arguments. However, if we are able to soldier through the unfamiliar literary conventions, we may reap the rich fruit of their solid Biblical theology. And it is quite a theology!

Thirdly, not every word in this canonical book should be taken as absolute Truth. Throughout the narrative, Job receives counsel from his three friends, and each conveys a particular theology. In the end, however, God rebukes the three friends for not speaking of Him rightly—unlike Job (42:7). Since God did not explain *how* Job's so-called friends were wrong, it is up to the reader to sort out their statements, separating truth from error.

This can be a daunting task, as a result there are few books in the Holy Scriptures that are as challenging to interpret.

Major Themes

The Book of Job is usually picked up and read in times of trouble. For most Christians, Job is a righteous man who perseveres through unimaginable suffering. But, surprisingly, suffering is not the main theme of the book. Suffering is just the backdrop for Job's devotion to be tested, and the readers become witnesses of a crisis. Job is challenged like a car being tested at its maximum acceleration. The test course for Job is a series of unheard of, shocking tragedies. There's one more character present on the scene—Satan. His goal is clearly stated: to create such road conditions that will cause the car to crash. He wants only one thing: for Job to curse his Creator so that he can prove to God that every man has his price—for some you pay more, for some less (2:4).

As a result, rather than focusing on Job's *suffering*, the Book of Job is concerned with Job's *unconditional devotion*, or devotion to God in the midst of trials. The whole narrative revolves around one question (or claim) of Satan: "Does Job fear God for nothing?" (1:9). The rest of the book is the refutation of this Satanic claim. There are also other themes in the book which we will discuss later. But its main structural framework is built upon this theme of unconditional devotion, and all the other truths depend on it.

Another major theme in the Book of Job is the meaning of life, which one of the most important topics one can consider and has been mulled over for millennia. When I think about this subject, I often use an illustration: imagine several hair dryers discussing their purpose in life. They sit and talk, they speculate, they express various points of view related to their life and purpose. And they each come up with different theories: to fly, to swim, to dig, to drive nails. In their madness, they forget to do the one important thing—read the manual in which their purpose is clearly stated. Every designer knows well in advance what he or she is designing. The same is true of the Bible; our Designer left us with clear teaching about our purpose in life. Yet, each generation comes up with their own purpose, ignoring "the instruction." In our time, there's a popular opinion belonging to such "hair dryers," who loudly proclaim that the meaning of life is to "follow your heart," "be true to yourself," and other platitudes. For those who only wish they could think less about difficult questions such as "why are we here?" this "wisdom" comes in handy. They may even spout these Hallmark greeting card sentiments in public to appear more intelligent or enlightened, while living as they had before.

The biblical teaching on the meaning of life may not seem attractive to many, but should we therefore look for "another" truth? Maybe we can try to accept this one as *the* truth, allowing it to fundamentally change our theology, thinking, feelings, behavior and, consequently, our lives? We will talk more about the meaning of life in later chapters. For now, let us look at Job.

Job's Life Before The Tragedy

Job's life was pleasing to the Lord; he was a spiritual giant compared to the rest of humanity. He knew earthly happiness, as it is understood by the majority of people. Can a man desire for more on this earth?

- He had plenty (he was wealthy) (1:3; 29:6);
- He had a happy family (1:2, 4; 29:5);

- He was respected and treated as an authority (1:3; 29:7–10);
- He was healthy (implied).

Job was phenomenally righteous and was blessed for that. The blessings were poured down on him in a continuous stream. Such a life was something he expected. Job kept the "instructions," and so he could expect the God of justice to be on his side and protect him from all possible trouble. After he had taken all the spiritual precautions, it would be inconceivable that one of Job's children should die, let alone all ten at once. He was even diligently offering sacrifices on behalf of his children after their parties just in case one of them might have silently cursed God in his or her heart. His sons and daughters must have lived in peace with each other, since they took regularly turns hosting family feasts in their homes (1:4). The most reasonable explanation for this familial bliss is Job's parental wisdom.

Tragedy

God was faithfully protecting Job from the Evil One. This was confirmed by Satan himself (1:10). But suddenly things changed; after a discussion (more like a wager) between God and Satan, the latter was allowed to turn the life of Job into hell on one condition—to spare his life (1:6–12; 2:1–6). In all other things, Satan was given a free hand to do with Job whatever his fiendish mind could conceive of (1:12; 2:6). At God's bidding, the angels retreated, the walls around Job were lifted up, leaving him at the mercy of, perhaps, the most powerful of all God-created spirits. Satan was granted power over everything that Job had—his wife, children, servants, flocks, possessions, even his health. And he didn't waste time taking full advantage of this opportunity. What happened next seems more like a nightmare than reality.

Job's children were all killed in a single blow. On the same day, all his flocks were destroyed, and he was left without any sustenance. Finally, Satan afflicted Job with an unknown skin disease (2:7). It doesn't really matter what type of disease it was, the point is that this righteous man was in great pain (2:7–8; 7:5, 14; 19:17; 30:17; 30:30). The life Job knew for many years was gone in an instant. Satan's strategy of choosing to attack Job on a day of family festivities reveals all his malice and hatred. The power of the fallen angel is demonstrated in the hideousness of his designs and their relentless implementation. However, God always puts a limit to his destructive powers, therefore we never can tell what exactly he is capable of (1:12; 2:6). We see that Satan is able to accomplish evil through other people; Sabeans and Chaldeans raided Job's land as if by arrangement (1:15, 17). What sort of tribes they were, where they lived or what languages they spoke is beside the point; what matters is that they did their black deed and got away with the plunder.

The description of the "fire from God" is also quite impressive, don't you think? It's hardly a description of earthly lightning (1:16). Lightening will usually hit one spot, killing rather than burning. According to the narrative, the fire from heaven fell and burnt a flock of seven thousand sheep spread over the area of thousands of square feet. Can you imagine that? It's more like a description of a colossal dragon breathing out fire, deliberately destroying every living thing in its path. It's not something one can easily forget. It is noteworthy that one of Job's messengers referred to it as fire "of God." In most ancient cultures, the sky was associated with dwelling, so since the fire fell from the sky, it must be from God, he concluded. Note that the fire from heaven also consumed the sheep, which were always considered sacrificial animals, even in pre-covenant times. It is very likely that Satan was trying "frame" God, doing everything in his power to make his cruelty look like the wrath of God. The destruction of the sacrificial animals could have be interpreted as God depriving Job of the very possibility to offer sacrifices and thus restore himself in His favor. Satan deliberately arranged the fire to look like righteous punishment. And this is exactly what Job concluded.

You can see here the insidiousness of the Devil's schemes. Messengers were coming to Job one by one, not allowing him time to even take a breath in between the bad news. But the biggest tragedy of all came the last, as if Job was given a chance to first feel the bitterness of smaller troubles before he was dealt the greatest blows; the death of all his children. But as we will soon see, it wasn't the last beating he took. This symphony of evil, so skillfully played by the Devil, remarkably demonstrates the vileness of his character and his great power. All the parts were masterfully played in good time—and by those who would never thought that they would perform in Satan's orchestra. And yet, against his own desire, Satan always plays to the tune of the Heavenly Director, following His sovereign theme impeccably as he is not allowed to go off pitch even by a half-note. This is a source of great consolation to all believers—God's sovereignty is one of the foundational doctrines of our faith.

God's Sovereignty

God is actively engaged in the trials that befall his saints. He is not a passive observer, but an initiator. Notice who initiated of the whole conversation about Job, when the angels first came into the presence of God. It was God! "Have you considered my servant Job?" This was God's question to Satan (1:8a). Why did he do it? Didn't He know that this exchange would lead to a wager? Of course He did! He was the One who had planned the wager in the first place. This was part of God's sovereign plan to fulfill His purposes. Does it mean that God Himself unleashed the deadly enemy having shown him his prey? Did He use His enemy as an instrument against the best of His servants? My answer is—yes. This is how it may seem at first, before we realize that God and Satan pursue different goals.

Consider this. The first question God asked of Satan when he made his first appearance before Him was: "From where do you come?" Why would the omniscient God ask that? Certainly, He knew where the adversary had been a moment ago and where he would be a moment after. He doesn't need Satan's answer—we do. Both times Satan's answer is the same, "Then Satan answered the Lord and said: 'From roaming about on the earth and walking around on it'" (1:7, 2:2). This is a warning to all of us so we know what our mortal enemy is up to during "business hours" (and I don't think he ever takes days off or goes on vacations). He is roaming about the earth, again and again. He circles around it! Why? Surely not to enjoy the scenery! Is he especially fond of traveling? Hardly. He's up to something! Our world is his sphere of interest. It is his "office." And he is doing what he is good at—seeking whom he may devour (1 Pet. 3:8). He's never weary of his job—he will trek around the world again and again. Notice this: the text assumes that Satan answered "yes" when the Lord had asked him about Job. He must have known about Job, and may have tried to harm him before. The only reason Satan didn't lay hands on Job before was because the Lord had protected him "on every side" (1:10). The Devil could not touch him.

And that is why *you* are still alive. God has put up a wall around you which you cannot see with physical eyes. Do you want to know what would happen if God took away this protection? Just look at Job. Things are not going so bad for you now not because Satan does not yet know about you. I am sure

Chapter 1. The Great Drama. Prologue

he already knows you by name, knows your strengths and weaknesses, your abilities and everything else there is to know, especially if you are a child of God. If he were allowed to, he would have gladly finished you right on the spot, without wasting time to torture you. He was a murderer from the beginning (John 8:44). The fact you are still alive means he is still bound. See how the Lord in his wisdom restrained Satan's actions toward Job: "Then the Lord said to Satan, 'Behold, all that he has is in your power, only do not put forth your hand on him.' So Satan departed from the presence of the Lord" (1:12). "So the Lord said to Satan, 'Behold, he is in your power, only spare his life'" (2:6).

Satan would never of his own free will spare someone who was handed over to him. He's bent on killing, and he will kill until he is restrained. He would not be content with less. All the good things in life that you experience are the result of restraining this most blood-thirsty being in the universe. He is muzzled. When I first realized this, I felt relief mixed with fear. I was relieved at the thought of all evil being kept on a short leash, but fear that this leash might be extended. We can, however, find comfort in knowing that God's actions are never arbitrary like the actions of a power-hungry tyrant; they are a wise governance of a father who wishes to bless to his children. "All the paths of the Lord are lovingkindness and truth to those who keep His covenant and His testimonies" (Ps. 25:10). Every situation is a part of His sovereign and perfect plan, which precludes anything accidental. His power, sovereignty and wisdom are seen in that our enemies' evil schemes are turned to our good. He uses even those who hate the children of God as channels of His blessings.

Are you able to see God behind everything that happens in your life? Do you realize that every "answer of the tongue" is from God, whether pleasant or not (Prov. 16:1)? You lost your job? It was God's doing. You did not get a new job? It was God who didn't let that happen. Someone you fell in love with rejected you? It was God's answer. Something was stolen from you? God took what was His in the first place. You got sick? This sickness came from God. All of life is perceived differently when it is seen through the lens of God's sovereignty. Accidents are ruled out. There is only predestination. Meaninglessness is ruled out. Everything is meaningful. Fear gives way to trust because the Almighty, the All-knowing and the All-loving *reigns!* He reigns even in the midst of injustice, cruelty and corruption because all of it is somehow part of His plan. His will is always done, and no one can stop it (42:2). Everything is foreseen, well-timed, and thought through.

God Cannot Be Controlled

We see a truth here that is hard to swallow; even righteous people can be severely tested. The lesson of Job is translucent; godliness is no guarantee of safety, whether in finance, health or family life. You may have also noticed that belonging to God yields no special privileges in this life. If you have been a believer for at least a year and you are honest with yourself, you know what I mean. There are always enough people out there who will insist on the "name and claim" theology. "We are children of the King!" What they usually mean is that royal children should live like royalty. If it doesn't happen, it must be because you have little faith. So, you should pray harder and claim more: "Give me, give me, give me!" It will go on as long as a person is successful enough in denying the obvious; God cannot be manipulated. You cannot pull His strings, He has none! In your relationship with God, there's no currency to buy God's good graces. There's no bargaining with God. Bargaining usually involves two conditions, mutual benefit and mutual obligation. What benefit can you give the One who gives you all the good things including your saving faith (Jam. 1:17; Phil. 1:29)? How can you oblige the One who owes you nothing and has no needs (Job 41:11; Rom. 11:35–36)?

An attempt to bargain with God is nothing but a form of religious manipulation. Every religion offers its ways to manipulate God—a method to trade with Heaven. Let's be honest, we all try to manipulate God to a certain degree. This is a propensity of our sinful flesh which we will carry until the day we die. Manipulation is our way to gain control. We see control as a key to attaining stability. It is this kind of stability that our fleshly mind understands as earthly bliss. Is there a power that can take away our stability in an instant? Of course. It is called God. So, we must gain control over this Power so as to avoid potential trouble. How can we do it? Easy. We need to figure out what God wants and exchange it for His favor. In other words, we must create a clear set of instructions on how to please God and stick to it! As I said earlier, every religion has its own God-pleasing instructions. Every religion claims to have the absolute *truth*, but most of them pursue one and the same goal—extracting as much earthly prosperity out of God as possible. Even Job tried to sort of manipulate God on a number of occasions.

> "His sons used to go and hold a feast in the house of each one on his day, and they would send and invite their three sisters to eat and drink with them. When the days of feasting had completed their cycle, Job would send and consecrate them, rising up early in the morning and offering burnt offerings according to the number of them all. For Job said, 'Perhaps my sons have sinned and cursed God in their hearts.' Thus Job did continually." (1:4–5)

It's important to realize that Job's sons were of age and would be responsible for their own actions, so they could offer their own sacrifices for their sins. If, for instance, Job's oldest son sinned in his heart, it would be between him and God to set things right, and that would have to be his son's initiative in the first place.

Now, human attempts to mediate between man and God aren't necessarily bad. For example, the priesthood was created to do just that. Praying for someone is also mediation. However, the attitude of someone you mediate for towards God remains crucial. By the way, Job did not know for sure if his children had sinned or not. So, in this case, he tried to *prevent* the trouble by offering sacrifices—to be on the safe side. *"Perhaps, my sons have sinned and cursed God in their hearts"* (1:5). It is, however, naive to conclude that God could be pleased with external rites of cleansing and external sacrifices without considering the person's heart. No doubt, God wanted to have personal relationships with Job's children, just as He had a relationship with their father. Job could not appease God for both himself and his children. It is humanly impossible. You may have heard a number of times that God has no grandchildren, He only has children. If one of Job's sons cursed God, that would have been his own responsibility to repent and bring sacrifices for his sin, not Job's. Of course, Job acted out of the best of intentions. As a father, he was trying to shield his whole family with his own godliness doing everything he could for them.

Can we judge him for this? I don't think so. He honestly believed that by offering sacrifices on behalf of his children, he pleased the Lord. Generally speaking, a person will do anything that religion requires of him in order to secure his own wellbeing. There's nothing wrong with getting good things here on earth, it is natural to expect God to protect you and help you. Isn't that what we expect from our earthly parents? But there is a distinct difference between expecting Fatherly protection and trying to wrap your Father around your finger. The Book of Job tells us that we are not able to insure ourselves against trouble by fasting, offering sacrifices, praying, being godly or learning theology. Obedience to God is no guarantee of earthly prosperity. In our world, true righteousness is not a shield from troubles, but rather a magnet that draws them. In this ancient book, God teaches that godliness should be an end in itself, not a way to get to something else. He teaches us that He cannot be manipulated—contrary to common pagan beliefs. This is one of the many differences between the true God and man-made idols. It would be impossible to invent such a God—He possesses all the characteristics which our sinful human flesh would resent. Our absolute inability to control Him is one of His main characteristics. People are afraid of sufferings, and many would gladly add God to their list of life resources, like a financial advisor or a bodyguard. They come to Him to secure His "saving services" trying to negotiate a contract with Him on their own terms. But sooner or later, we find out He's not a puppet, especially so when tragedy strikes.

In times of trial, we become aware of where our true treasure is. God sees what is in the heart of man (Prov. 15:11). Self-deception is a human thing. It may seem to us that we would follow Christ to whatever end, we think we are firm in our faith, and that we worship Him gladly. But we often do not see that our peace of mind, joy, humility and even faith are based upon a relatively comfortable lifestyle. When a hurricane strikes, all the chaff of our fleshly righteousness is blown away, the fog of self-deception has dissipated, and the rotten pillars of our Christianity crumble. God and man come face to face—no more delusions. Everything is crystal clear. Are we going to worship God when He "acts out," or will we shake our fists at the heavens? It's easy to make fine speeches about our devotion to God and His perfections. But the most practical of answers to this question will come the day we face sufferings. You can only truly know yourself and what you are capable of after going through hard times. Trials reveal the quality of our faith. This is the only way to know what is inside a man, and to honestly answer the question "Why do I need God?"

> *What is the hope of the godless when he is cut off,*
> *when God required his life?*
> *Will God hear his cry*
> *when distress comes upon him?*
> *Will he take delight in the Almighty?*
> *Will he call on God at all times?*
> *(Job 27:8–10)*

2
THEOLOGICAL
DIFFICULTIES

To better understand what was happening to Job at the time of his suffering, to understand his complaints was well as the power of the blow dealt to his faith, it is necessary to assess the theology he adhered to. It is clear that, beginning with the third chapter of the story, Job's heart bursts open. He can no longer remain silent, pretending that these events somehow make any sense. Far from it. Nothing makes sense! And the reason for this is his theology, based on his convictions at that time, was not able to help in correctly interpreting the situation.

First of all, any theology asks the question "Who is God?" and in the process of searching for an answer, a picture is gradually formed in a person's mind about God's character, His qualities, abilities, commands, and intentions. In other words, the person gets some idea of who God is. When trouble overtook this righteous man, Job had known God to the degree that God had revealed Himself. Job believed that God acted on the basis of certain qualities of His character. In other words, he possessed some kind of "systematic theology" of the Creator, as can be inferred from his own statements. This also means that at that time he had a set of theological beliefs, by which he interpreted the actions of the Lord in relation to himself and others. However, the process of interpretation became really difficult after he found himself in this highly unusual situation. But before we take a closer look at his difficulties, we need to say a few words about the epistemological aspect of any theology, namely, the source of our knowledge of God.

The Source of Truth

The question "Who is God?" is closely connected to another question: how do we know what God is like? If there is a revelation of God about Himself, then there must be a way in which this revelation was received. There is enough evidence to conclude that Job lived in the time of the patriarchs—before the covenant between God and Israel was made. As far as we know, there was no recorded revelation from God at that time, from which people could draw their theology. If it existed, it would be reasonable to expect that during their extensive theological debate, Job or his friends would appeal to some sort of solid canon, or "code." But we don't see any such references. Instead, they most often referred to their own or someone else's spiritual experience, common sense, and, probably, to oral traditions. Job mentions certain "words of the Holy One," which he did not deny (6:10). It can be stated with certainty that Job and his friends were quite limited in this regard, and most importantly, they were more vulnerable in the process of developing their own theologies. If someone came along and said that he had received revelation from the Lord, like

Eliphaz the Temanite (4:12), how could this be verified? There was only one way to test it—time. But even before it became clear whether the person was a true prophet or an imposter, it was necessary to decide whether to believe him or not, because he was rebuking, commanding, calling to action, or warning about something, which would either need to be obeyed or rejected. As a result, we may conclude that in the past believers were much more prone to all kinds of misconceptions about God than they would be today.

In our times, God reveals Himself in the pages of the Holy Scriptures, and this is our highest privilege, because it is the only reliable way to know His will and character. The written Word undermines all self-imposed religious activity. It rises above intuitions, feelings, and spiritual experiences, whether our own or someone else's. In chapter three, we will see how Job's friends share with him their visions, "prophecies," and spiritual revelations, but it becomes obvious that for such a wealth of "God-knowing tools" their theology is false and shaky. I found it quite interesting that, according to Job, he had never received a single vision or personal revelation from God prior to his sufferings (42:5a). However, his faith was as strong as steel, and he was one of the most revered righteous men on earth. To top it off, in the midst of this incredible chaos, he was able to speak of God what was right, unlike his friends with their so-called "revelations" (42:7). The conclusions are obvious.

In our day, many Christians would say that to preach the uniqueness of Scripture as the only source of special revelation limits God. For some reason, it seems to them that the character of God's revelation would be terribly impoverished if the revelation was regulated exclusively to the Bible. "What about the voice of the Holy Spirit?" they ask. "What about prophecies, visions and dreams? If there were personal revelations in the past, why can't we have them now?" Such questions can only be asked by people for whom the Scripture remains a closed book. I do not wish to offend anyone, but judge for yourself; if you do not find in the Bible all the necessary guidance for your daily walk with God, if you prefer to make decisions by closing your eyes, sticking your finger on a random page of the Bible, or listening "prayerfully" to what you think the Holy Spirit might be saying to you, this only confirms your inability to properly use this precious book. When these "religious" methods of divining God's will inevitably fail to produce the desired results, these confused Christians throw up their hands in frustration and don't open their Bibles again. As a result, neglected Bibles around the world are gathering dust on the shelves of many Christian homes. Instead of diligently studying the Word of God, Christians eagerly seek human revelations. Instead of learning from the Scriptures "what is the good, acceptable and perfect will of God," many are looking for prophecies, dreams, signs and visions. The believers who lived in the times of Job can be justified since they had nothing else to rely on, but there's no excuse for modern-day believers. Possessing the perfect, complete, reliable, effective, ocean-deep, understandable Word of God, they are sadly still looking for new "prophecies."

In Job's time, believers did not have the luxury of turning to the Scriptures for guidance. What is amazing is that his friends' theology was not at all primitive. They had more or less of a clear idea of how to live righteously before God and had some understanding of His nature. They knew something about the works of the Lord, and they interpreted His actions through the lens of their theology—whether in their own lives or in the lives of other people. You see, interpreting God's actions is part and parcel of every theology, because His works are always rooted in His nature. Each divine act proceeds from His qualities and our actions proceed from ours; Jesus pointed out that a man's actions are an unmistakable indicator of what is in his heart (Matt. 7:16–20). In other words, your actions reveal who you are.

While this is true about people, it cannot be directly applied to God, for the works of the Lord do not easily lend themselves to such an interpretation. For example, when God allows evil to touch us, it does not mean that He is evil or unjust. There is no correlation there, although for a human mind, corrupted by sin, such a claim would seem like an abyss of logical inconsistency. And this abyss can only be crossed by the bridge of faith. Logic is useless here. As He tells us in Isaiah, "For my thoughts are not your thoughts, nor are your ways My ways," declares the Lord. "For as heavens are higher than the earth, so are My ways higher than your ways and My thoughts than your thoughts" (Is. 55:8–9). At the very least, this passage tells us that our thinking is very different from God's. It also means that what we think of as natural, normal and logically sound, can be something totally different for God.

It is hardly necessary for me to argue that objectivity belongs to God, not to man. Therefore, the actions of the Creator should not be interpreted so much by our reasoning as by His Word whenever possible. God must be allowed to explain His own action. We should not try to do it for Him, because, as we can see in the example of Job's friends, such attempts are futile. Sadly, there are those in our churches who take it upon themselves to judge the works of God according to their own understanding, as if they know for sure what He is up to. My brother in Christ got in an accident? He did not pray before the trip. Her husband has not yet repented? The wife did not share enough of the gospel with him. Someone's sister got sick? She was in rebellion, etc. In other words, people feel that there must be some cause-and-effect correlation between the person's actions and the events in his life, but they do not realize that such a correlation is often beyond our interpretation.

Job and his friends had a theology that was based on such a cause-and-effect worldview. The unfolding of this law in the spiritual realm is expressed in the Scriptures through the principle of sowing and reaping, "Whatever a man sows, that he will also reap" (Gal. 6:7). The presence of causality in the world, which can be observed at all levels of the created cosmos, is the result of order in the universe. Order, as opposed to chaos, is the totality of the unchanging laws on which the world is built. Job and his friends understood perfectly well that order is inherent in God's nature. They rightly believed that, because of this intrinsic orderliness in the nature of God, His actions must be either predictable, or understandable and reasonable in some sense. Just as an object is expected to fall down due to the law of gravity, so the actions of God must be explainable through some laws—namely, through the qualities inherent in His nature. And that's where our main characters ran into theological problems. The tragedy simply could not be explained in terms of cause and effect. Such a thing could happen to anyone but Job!

The Unpredictable God

Even though God Himself called Job the first righteous man on earth, Job had another lesson to learn. This lesson has been a blessing to all believers for thousands of years, and for this very reason it was recorded, just as Job wanted (Job 19:23). According to human logic, if anyone needed such a drastic spiritual overhaul, it wasn't Job. Yet what Job feared, what he didn't expect, came upon him (3:25). He encountered a side of God he did not yet know. What happened did not fit his theology because his theology did not allow for that to happen. Poor Job could not reconcile his beliefs about God with God's actions, which increased his already unbearable suffering. There was only one formula in Job's theology to explain such horrendous circumstances, which was incidentally shared by his friends: Sin + unwillingness to repent = punishment (4:7–9). Job did not have any other way to account for what was happening to him. He interpreted the reality using the formula he already had (a + b = c). The result "c" (the tragedy) was already there, so he only had to find the components "a" and "b" from which this result was derived. In other words, since the whole situation fell under the definition of "punishment" according to this logic, Job had no other choice but to answer the question: why? So, he began to search. And as he was searching for an answer, he started looking back at his past. Finally, it occurred to him that, perhaps, God remembered the sins of his younger self. "For you write bitter things against me and make me to inherit the iniquities of my youth" (13:26).

But why so late and, more importantly, why so harsh? Job was sure that even in the relatively frivolous time of his youth, he did not do anything that would merit such treatment. Throughout the book, he argues that he led a blameless life. Honest self-analysis ended with a fair conclusion, ". . . till I die I will not put away my integrity from me. I hold fast to my righteousness and will not let it go. My heart does not reproach any of my days" (27:5–6). The verdict Job gave himself was innocent, but it was this very verdict intensified his desperation because no logical explanation for the tragedy was to be found. If he had found what he had been punished for, everything would have fallen into place, and his theology would not have changed. But the situation looked so desperate precisely because Job had done *nothing* to warrant such punishment. The Lord himself testified to this, immediately dismissing all suspicions on the part of the reader that His actions in relation to Job might be characterized as punishment:

> "The Lord said to Satan, "Have you considered My servant Job? For there is no one like him on the earth, a blameless and upright man, fearing God and turning away from evil." (1:8)

> "The Lord said to Satan, "Have you considered My servant Job? For there is no one like him on the earth, a blameless and upright man fearing God and turning away from evil. And he still holds fast his integrity, although you incited Me against him to ruin him without cause." (2:3)

Job's theology predicted a totally different outcome on the basis of the aforementioned formula. This time it was expressed in different words: good works + good works = prosperity. The formula worked wonderfully all his life until it failed. It was a shock, much like a chef would be shocked if he was making soup from the best vegetables and the choicest meats, but his dish turned out to be rancid. Or like a farmer who sowed wheat, but reaped a rich crop of poison ivy. What else could that mean but not a sudden and unimaginable change in the very laws of nature? Job could not understand how it was possible to reap such horrendous evil, when all his life he was sowing nothing but good. How could God do such a thing?! It felt as if the foundations of the world crumbled—the very foundations of which he firmly believed.

Growing in the knowledge God is a process. God will from time to time reveal Himself in ways which were previously hidden from us or were above our understanding. A difficult passage in the Bible will suddenly make sense; a question that you have long struggled will all of a sudden get a clear answer. Some past or present event will immediately appear in a completely different light, revealing to your mind a totally new facet of the character of God. A person's narrow theology is expanded as he embraces yet another truth about God. Every Christian has questions, the answers to which lie beyond the limits of our earthly existence. Some of them will not be answered in this life at all. On the earthly plane, the nature of God and His actions cannot be entirely comprehended by the limited human mind, corrupted by sin.

The mind is a poor helper when it comes to the knowledge of God—that is, if faith is not thrown into the mix, as previously mentioned. Moreover, in the absence of faith, your mind can become your enemy and hinder your knowledge of God. Let me give an example: if you were a general commanded to march against an army of thousands with just three hundred men, what would your logical mind tell you? This is suicide! But add faith to the equation, and everything will immediately change, because now you have the Almighty in the picture. Or if you were a young unarmed shepherd going against a giant clad in chainmail and wielding a sword, what would your mind say? "I should have left a will." But add faith to the equation, and your vision would change; the one who was helpless turned into a mighty warrior, and the mighty champion turned into a weakling.

This is what faith does! This was what saved Job when his mind was helpless. After an honest and thorough analysis of everything that had happened, he still had no answers, but faith, his precious faith, strengthened his feeble knees and led him on through the impenetrable darkness of the inexplicable. His faith was his only friend that he could rely on in the toughest of trials. When everything else failed, faith did not. It did not cease. It was gently but firmly unclenching his fingers when Job was tempted to shake his fists against Heaven. But first, faith had to survive the crisis.

The Crisis of Theology

There is no faith without theology! It is the content of our faith. Listening to Job's speeches, we understand that this righteous man's spiritual torment was proceeding mainly from his faulty theology which was falling apart under the pressure of unanswered questions. After all, he also knew the same God of justice his friends so vehemently promoted. And now his whole worldview was shaken to the core. The crisis hit suddenly. It was the turning point of his entire life. The trouble would either make him or break him (like it broke his wife). Job was genuinely frightened that God may have turned away from him. But if that were the case, it wouldn't be so bad because you can always repent and find forgiveness with a merciful God. The real trouble was that as a devout believer, he was always ready to repent, but could not understand what to repent *of!* Everything that had happened looked very much like punishment, so his main question to God throughout the narrative was: "Why?" "I will say to God, 'Do not condemn me; let me know why You contend with me'" (10:2). "How many are my iniquities and sins? Make known to me my rebellion and my sin" (13:23). True, what happened did not fit any theological formula he knew, but at the time Job did not yet realize that it was time to learn a new one.

Job didn't know that his theology would soon take a huge leap, and that his despair would dissipate forever. Job concluded that the suffering that came upon him was not deserved (27:6). And since it was not deserved, another scary question had to be answered; "If I am suffering unjustly, can God be just?" This question clung to his mind, and finally he voiced it. In his desperation, this righteous man makes a reckless statement, putting God on trial. Again and again he states his desire: "But I would speak to the Almighty, and I desire to argue with God" (13:3). "Though He slay me, I will hope in Him" (13:15). "Behold now, I have prepared my case; I know that I will be vindicated" (13:18).

On the one hand, he simply wants to appeal his case to the Judge—maybe there's been some mistake! Maybe his case could be reconsidered! "Oh that I knew where I might find Him, that I might come to His seat! I would present my case before Him and fill my mouth with arguments. I would learn the words which He would answer and perceive what He would say to me" (23:3–5).

Job wanted the Judge of the universe to rise up from His throne and come down so he could plead his case as if God were a person, "O that a man might plead with God as a man with his neighbor!" (16:21). To wish for such a thing is to assume that the case could be won, and that the judge could become a defendant. As crazy as it sounds, that's exactly what some believers do. When we find ourselves in dire straits where we cannot explain some of God's actions, we do the most stupid thing imaginable—start doubting His justice, wisdom, love, and other qualities. In other words, we make God the suspect. It is a futile and dangerous business. And it is a shocking idea that imperfection can question perfection. Job did just that—challenged God's justice.

Unable to explain the cause of his torments, he sinned, like most suffering people, by attacking the character of God. "For He bruises me with a tempest and multiplies my wounds without cause. He will not allow me to get my breath, but saturates me with bitterness" (9:17–18). "Though I am righteous, my mouth will condemn me; though I am guiltless, He will declare me guilty. I am guiltless; I do not take notice of myself; I despise my life" (9:20–21). At the brink of despair, he concludes that there's no use in being righteous. It will not shield you from trouble in this life. And, as you may have noticed (9:20), he accuses God of partiality in judgement. As he continues his ruminations, he comes to utter hopelessness, "It is all one; therefore I say, He destroys the guiltless and the wicked" (9:22). "I am accounted wicked, why then should I toil in vain? If I should wash myself with snow and cleanse my hands with lye, yet You would plunge me into the pit, and my own clothes would abhor me" (9:29–31).

Up to this moment, Job believed that his righteousness was his shield from trouble. Now he had to reconcile his faith in the just God with the fact that He "destroys the guiltless and the wicked." Now that his super-righteousness did not save him from tragedy (as he had hoped), he had a natural question—if I was found guilty, why am I still following the path of righteousness? His human concept of God's justice was shattered to pieces, "Behold, I cry, 'Violence!' but I get no answer; I shout for help, but there is no justice. He has walled up my way so that I cannot pass, and He has put darkness on my paths" (19:7–8).

God's Justice

Just like Job, people will usually question God's justice when they personally go through hard times or when trouble comes to their loved ones. Even the first murderer in the history of the world did not hesitate to accuse God of injustice when justly punished for his iniquity (Gen. 4:13–14). This was one of the first accusation of the Creator pronounced by mankind. The sufferer is so fixated on justice because he has his own idea of what it should be. We could say Cain is comparing what is with what should be according to his own understanding. Then, turning to God, he points out some specific circumstances in his life and demands that justice should be restored.

What should we do when we are tempted, like Job, to accuse God of injustice? How should we act, what should we think and remember? Let me offer you four truths that will help you overcome the temptation. The first and the foremost truth from the Bible is that God calls Himself just. Let us remember that. "Righteousness and justice are the foundation of Your throne; Lovingkindness and truth go before You" (Ps. 89:14). "For I, the Lord, love justice, I hate robbery in the burnt offering" (Is. 61:8). God's own in itself is a sufficient reason for us to stop doubting and start trusting Him.

In other words, we have a simple choice: take the Holy One at His word or call Him a liar. What do you think about this choice? Sad as it is, many of us require additional evidence of God's justice and other divine qualities. His words are not enough for us! But do you know that the Word of God is the final argument against such doubts? If the Bible is not able to convince us, then mark my words, nothing else will do. God Himself speaks to us through His Word. God Himself is forming our theology, and He uses His words as bricks. When we read the Bible, God talks to us personally. And if this is so, who is able to speak more convincingly than God Himself? Whose words are more powerful? Woe to us if we require proof for the words of the Lord. All of our disputes with the Lord usually boil down to the following dialogue:

God: Trust Me, I am just.

Man: Prove it.

God: Can you trust Me first? Then I will prove it.

Man: No, first prove it, then I will trust You.

But is this faith? Faith is the assurance of things hoped for, the conviction of things not seen (Heb. 11:1). When we see, it's not faith. Perhaps someone would say, "Yes, but actions speak louder than words." I would reply that this is a fatal mistake. It is true that actions speak louder than words, but not in your relationship with God which is based on faith. Faith stands on the foundation of biblical truths and comes from hearing the Word—not from seeing. If receiving the most important thing in the world, your salvation, requires trusting in the Word of God (Rom. 10), why would growing in holiness require something else?

Read the parable of Jesus about the rich man and Lazarus (Luke 16:19–31). We can argue about the interpretation of this parable, but for now let us focus on one thing. It is clearly stated in verse 31 that Scripture is the main factor in converting the sinner. The rich man, who is in hell, asks Abraham to send Lazarus back to his family. He believes that if his brothers saw such a miracle, they would certainly turn to God and escape this place of perdition. But Abraham replies that seeing the miracle performed by God would not help them believe. The only thing necessary for faith is the Word of God, and they already have that. They have the writings of Moses and the prophets. The rich man objects, insisting that the works of the Lord would speak louder than His written Word. Through Abraham, Jesus makes a very important statement; if a person would not believe through the testimony of the Bible, miracles are of no help to him. This statement confirms that the highest authority and power belongs to the Word of God. In matters of faith, the authority of the Word of God is superior to the authority of God's actions. So, do not think that God has to prove to you that He is just. Do not ask Him to earn your trust by acting a certain way. Learn to take Him at his word. ". . . Your word is truth" (John 17:17).

Secondly, to avoid the temptation of accusing God of injustice, we must agree that there is something fundamentally wrong, even from the purely logical point of view, for a limited and imperfect creature to judge the infinite and perfect Creator. We have no ability measure the actions of someone who is perfect. Our minds simply cannot grasp the mosaic of Providence, formed by intersection of events, life's subtle intricacies and apparent "coincidences." We do not have the mental capacity to comprehend God's sovereign plan for everything that happens in the universe. Trusting Him is the only way.

Thirdly, let us admit that when we complain about something "unfair" in our lives, it usually means that our plans were thwarted. We had spent so much time crafting a perfect scenario for our lives, then prayed diligently for God to approve it and bring it about (in the name of Christ, of course), but something went wrong. Other people's plans succeeded, ours didn't. And you know what amazes me the most? That our internal "unfairness sensor" seems to only go off when our situation in life turns from good to worse. As long as our lives are slowly improving, everything is "yes" and "amen." Life is fair. But the moment things get hard, we go out into the streets to protest against the "injustice." I have never met a person who would complain about God being unfair in blessing them. When everything is fine, we don't say, "Lord, don't you see I don't deserve this? This isn't fair. Please take me a step back down." This would be unheard of.

One of my friends did the following experiment on his two children. Dividing a piece of cake into three parts, he gave two pieces to his daughter, and one to his son. The son quickly protested, "It's not fair!" Then the father took the second piece from his daughter and gave it to the son. His daughter similarly claimed that the situation was unfair. So, he gave her back what she demanded, and sure enough, the son immediately got upset. My friend repeated these "cake manipulations" several times, and then he had them sit down in front of him and asked why they were so upset when one of them had more than the other. The answer came right away; it's not fair. It's not fair when someone has two pieces, and the other person has one. "Well," said the father, "why then didn't you cry 'not fair' when you had two pieces, and your sister had only one?" The son looked bewildered. He asked his daughter the same question, but got no intelligible answer. According to his story, the children could not even understand what he was talking about. He also had a hard time explaining to them that they were being inconsistent. For them, "not fair" worked in one direction only—when *someone else* had more than they did. Don't you recognize yourself here? Don't we all act like these children?

Finally, see what happens when this logic is applied to our salvation. Is it "fair" for Jesus, who was sinless, to die for us, sinners? Among those who received salvation, none will demand to be sent to hell to pay for his sins. Think about it—we are totally fine with such an unfair treatment. It is important for us to see that our human concept of justice is very subjective and one-sided.

Our internal compass of justice gets constantly reoriented towards our personal benefit. Our personal benefit is the very foundation of our understanding of universal justice. Let us wholeheartedly embrace the biblical truth that God is just and let us not follow the example of Job who tried to put God on trial. Demanding justice from God means accusing Him of injustice. Such a demand is both sinful and unrealistic; it is sinful because it is an expression of unbelief and unrealistic because God does not give account for His actions. Job challenged God's character. He explained his tragedy through the assumption that the Creator of the Universe is unjust. Job's theology offered no other theories for interpreting the troubles he was going through. His friends, however, had their own explanation.

> *Why do you complain against Him*
> *that He does not give an account of all His doings?*
> *(Job 33:13)*

3

THE MISERABLE COMFORTERS

In the previous chapter, we discussed some of the theological problems that Job faced. Now let's take a closer look at his three friends and analyze their theological convictions. Job described them as "miserable comforters" (16:2, NIV), and he had every reason to do so. Let's try to understand why the counseling they offered failed so miserably.

The second chapter of the book of Job tells us about his three friends, who, having heard about his tragedy, came to support him and to show sympathy. "Now when Job's three friends heard of all this adversity that had come upon him, they came each one from his own place, Eliphaz the Temanite, Bildad the Shuhite and Zophar the Naamathite; and they made an appointment together to come to sympathize with him and comfort him" (2:11). Note their original goal—"to sympathize with him and comfort him." The first week they just sat with him silently on the ground, in the dust, with their clothes torn, probably not knowing what to say or what to do. Job was silent too. As it turned out later, this was the best consolation that they offered him in his misery (13:4–5). It is not clear what role they would have played in this story if Job did not start pouring out his heart before them. Having listened to him, the friends decided to break the silence; their very first words show that they didn't like what they heard. They were very angry. Isn't fair to ask what did the unfortunate sufferer say that made them so upset? Let's find out.

It should be noted that these trials were a test for Job's friends as well. They also had a hard time because all these events dealt a devastating blow to their own convictions. But what they initially saw shocked them to the core. What?! This happened to Job?! It can't be! Why? He is not that kind of person! This could have happened to anyone but to this paragon of righteousness, there must be a mistake! The terrible sight that they saw did not square well with their idea of a just God and a righteous Job. As believers, they had to somehow reconcile what had happened with their cause-and-effect theology. But knowing Job's blamelessness, they were at a loss. It wasn't easy, yet they finally did it. They found an "explanation" for the causes of the tragedy, but to do so they had to go against their consciences. They thought they found an answer, sort of. So, what was this answer?

A White Lie

Using deductive reasoning, their reflections can be briefly summarized as God does not punish the innocent (4:7), Job has been severely punished by God (11:6), therefore, Job is guilty (22:5). It's that simple, and that logical. The theological conundrum is solved. Oh, how gladly they would have pushed their Creator back into the box from which He almost escaped. After all, it is very uncomfortable to live with the knowledge that the Lord could do such a terrible thing to one of the godliest men alive. No, they thought, this can't be. It just means that the righteous man is not so righteous, otherwise the Lord Most High would not have struck him. The God they knew would not have allowed all the children of the innocent man to perish at once. The God they knew would not have inflicted such a terrible disease on a righteous man. The God they knew would not have plunged a godly man into poverty. Therefore, their counseling was mainly this—repent of the sin that has brought upon you such a calamity. They were trying to help him, but they didn't; they only aggravated the sufferings of their dear friend, and in the end barely escaped God's punishment for their moralizing.

A brief analysis of the type of counseling these miserable comforters offered helps us to not to repeat their mistake when we are called by God to become comforters for someone. They did at least four things wrong, three of which have to do with telling lies.

The First Mistake—Lying About God
Job's friends made theological statements that were ungrounded. Apparently, they wanted to disprove the arguments of the opposing party so much that they resorted to wishful thinking. And this is what mainly caused the wrath of God against them. "It came about after the Lord had spoken these words to Job, that the Lord said to Eliphaz the Temanite, 'My wrath is kindled against you and against your two friends, because you have not spoken of Me what is right as My servant Job has'" (42:7). In their inordinate desire to prove their point, they crossed the fine line between what is permissible and what is not, and just invented a God based on their own theological fabrications, passing them off as generally accepted truths. We need to carefully study the speeches of Job's friends, now that we know that not everything they said was

true. God allowed for their words to be recorded in the Bible, but He also warned us that what they were saying about Him may not be accurate. At the same time, we must admit that much of what they said was sound doctrine. It seems interesting that their misconceptions about God were a much more serious problem in the eyes of God than all the things they said correctly—even more serious than Job's complaints. We see that God specifically focused on the negative part of their poor counseling, leaving without a single comment all the "correct" things they said. Let us find in the text what exactly the Creator was so angry about.

Eliphaz:

"Can mankind be just before God? Can a man be pure before his Maker? He puts no trust even in His servants; and against His angels He charges error. 'How much more those who dwell in houses of clay, whose foundation is in the dust, who are crushed before the moth!" (4:17–19)

Eliphaz claimed that these thoughts were not his own. He had, allegedly, received these words as a personal revelation. The description of how he received this revelation makes me think that he wasn't being honest. Let's read starting with verse 12:

"Now a word was brought to me stealthily, and my ear received a whisper of it. Amid disquieting thoughts from the visions of the night, when deep sleep falls on men, dread came upon me, and trembling, and made all my bones shake. Then a spirit passed by my face; the hair of my flesh bristled up. It stood still, but I could not discern its appearance; a form was before my eyes; there was silence, then I heard a voice." (4:12–16)

The described process of obtaining this revelation is very different from other similar situations in the Word of God. First, note the uncertainty of the source. "Now a word was brought to me stealthily . . ." Whoever brought the word didn't introduce himself. It's very strange. To tell you the truth, the "secret revelations" that come to modern-day believers can be so annoying. Given the seriousness of the situation (every revelation is serious business), there should have been some sort of introduction before the word was given, so that there would be no doubt as to the source of the revelation (Ex. 3:6). But no introduction was given. Secondly, there was visual uncertainty. Based on the description, it could have been an angel or a demon. ". . . But [Eliphaz] could not discern its appearance; a form was before my eyes . . ." When the Lord gives a revelation, He makes sure that the messenger's identity is discernible, just a voice would have been more than enough, as often happened in the Old Testament (1 Sam. 3; Acts 9:4). Whenever God appeared to someone personally or sent His angels as messengers, everything was very discernible and could easily be described. Thirdly, note the uncertainty of the addressee. Who was the revelation for? If it was intended for Eliphaz, it seems too fragmented, without a beginning or an end, and it sounds irrelevant. If it was for Job, why didn't Eliphaz know about it? The Lord always informed his prophets as to whom His message was addressed (Ex. 3:14; Lev. 1:2; 2 Sam. 7:8; Is. 38:5). Fourthly, the nature of the "revelation" seems suspiciously similar to the theological views of Eliphaz himself.

Fifthly (and most importantly), the very content of the "revelation" directly contradicts the assessment of Job's character by God. This assessment does not mean that Job was sinless (Job 1:8b). It's just a confirmation that God was pleased with Job. Besides, in all of Scripture we do not find even one verse to support the claim "He puts no trust even in His servants" and "against His angels He charges error." The Holy One will not tolerate the presence someone who is unclean in His sight (Rev. 21:27). Apparently, Eliphaz was so eager to convince Job that he was sinful, and that God was holy, that Eliphaz almost made a fool of himself in the process. In my opinion, he simply invented a "revelation"—without a twinge of conscience, as sometimes happens among believers today.

In another passage, he says something even more appalling, "Is there any pleasure to the Almighty if you are righteous, Or profit if you make your ways perfect?" (Job 22:3). This statement directly contradicts the truth of Scripture. The Lord is pleased when people lead holy lives. Eliphaz claimed that it doesn't matter to God how a person lives. He calls the Creator indifferent, and this is not true. We see in God's Word that sin causes the Lord to feel wrath and sorrow, but righteous acts are a joy to Him (8:20–21; 2 Sam. 12:13–14; Is. 43:21–24; Luke 19:41–44). Human life is inseparably connected to the glory of the Creator, and everything that we do is somehow related to His glory. And when it comes to His glory, the Lord is very jealous and takes things seriously. That's why He is pleased with obedience and displeased with disobedience (Num. 14:29; Matt. 25:21; Luke 15:7; Rom. 1:18). Regardless of what Eliphaz imagined, God is not separate from humanity in that way, and whatever came from his lips isn't the best teaching on the transcendence[1] of the Creator.

Eliphaz is just as reckless in his statements elsewhere, "What is man, that he should be pure, or he who is born of a woman, that he should be righteous? Behold, He puts no trust in His holy ones, and the heavens are not pure in His sight" (15:14–15). Bildad echoes his words, "How then can a man be just with God? Or how can he be clean who is born of woman? If even the moon has no brightness and the stars are not pure in His sight" (25:4–6). Scripture testifies to the Lord's positive assessment of His own work after the creation of the world, "God saw all that He had

---

[1] Transcendence is a theological concept describing God as "separate" from His creation.

made, and behold, it was very good" (Gen. 1:31a). This means that God did not leave anything unfinished: not the stars, nor the heavens, nor any other part of the creation. Can the Lord choose something unclean as a foundation of His throne (Is. 66:1)? Can He surround Himself with the "holy ones" who He doesn't trust? How can His "holy ones" be called "holy" if they are not pure? And how can the stars not be pure if they are inanimate objects? In their eagerness to emphasize the infinite gap between the perfection of the Creator and the imperfections of creation, Eliphaz and Bildad were inventing beautiful, but exaggerated analogies and metaphors, speaking of things they didn't fully understand. Zophar quickly caught up with his friends by driving a couple of nails into the lid of Job's coffin,

> "But would that God might speak, and open His lips against you, and show you the secrets of wisdom! For sound wisdom has two sides. Know then that God forgets a part of your iniquity." (Job 11:5–6)

Zophar seems to imply that the punishment was not severe enough. He believes it could have been more severe if God had decided to repay Job for all his sins. No doubt, one needs a lot of self-control to tolerate such a statement like this from a dear friend. Considering the circumstances, it was quite impressive that Job didn't spit in his face. I would ask Zophar a simple question—how does he imagine greater punishment than what Job already suffered?

The Second Mistake—Lying About How The World Is
Job's friends deliberately distorted reality as we know it just to prove their point. From their perspective, righteousness and justice always have the upper hand. They claim that all the sinners receive their due in this life, and all the righteous live happily

ever after. But this is a lie! Trying to defend God's justice, they painted before Job a portrait of the "average" sinner, doomed to trouble and perdition. The only problem is that this portrait looks very much like Job—with all the unique circumstances of his life mentioned. Keep in mind Job's situation as you read the following accusations by Job's friends:

Eliphaz:

"Remember now, who ever perished being innocent? Or where were the upright destroyed? According to what I have seen, those who plow iniquity and those who sow trouble harvest it. By the breath of God they perish, and by the blast of His anger they come to an end." (4:7–9)

"Please inquire of past generations, and consider the things searched out by their fathers. For we are only of yesterday and know nothing, because our days on earth are as a shadow.[2] Will they not teach you and tell you, and bring forth words from their minds? Can the papyrus grow up without a marsh? Can the rushes grow without water? While it is still green and not cut down, yet it withers before any other plant. So are the paths of all who forget God; and the hope of the godless will perish." (8:8–13)

"The wicked man writhes in pain all his days, and numbered are the years stored up for the ruthless. Sounds of terror are in his ears; while at peace the destroyer comes upon him. He does not believe that he will return from darkness, and he is destined for the sword. He wanders about for food, saying, 'Where is it?' He knows that a day of darkness is at hand. Distress and anguish terrify him, they overpower him like a king ready for the attack." (15:20–24)

---

[2] An indication that the lifespan of Job's contemporaries was cut short. This is an indirect evidence that the time of the patriarchs was near.

"He has lived in desolate cities, in houses no one would inhabit, which are destined to become ruins. He will not become rich, nor will his wealth endure; and his grain will not bend down to the ground." (15:28–29)

Bildad:

"His skin is devoured by disease, the firstborn of death devours his limbs." (18:13)

"He has no offspring or posterity among his people, nor any survivor where he sojourned. Those in the west are appalled at his fate, and those in the east are seized with horror." (18:19–20)

"Do you know this from of old, from the establishment of man on earth, that the triumphing of the wicked is short, and the joy of the godless momentary?" Though his loftiness reaches the heavens, and his head touches the clouds, He perishes forever like his refuse; those who have seen him will say, 'Where is he?'" (20:4–7)

"In the fullness of his plenty he will be cramped; the hand of everyone who suffers will come against him. When he fills his belly, God will send His fierce anger on him and will rain it on him while he is eating." (20:22–23)

"The heavens will reveal his iniquity, and the earth will rise up against him. The increase of his house will depart; his possessions will flow away in the day of His anger. This is the wicked man's portion from God, even the heritage decreed to him by God." (20:27–29)

Isn't it true, that all of these things sound like something they could have been invented spontaneously by just looking at the fate of a friend. From the very beginning, they resorted to lies and hypocrisy, forgetting about the fear of God. But Job figured out what was going on, and, after the first round of accusations, exposed them as liars:

> "Will you speak what is unjust for God, and speak what is deceitful for Him? Will you show partiality for Him? Will you contend for God? Will it be well when He examines you? Or will you deceive Him as one deceives a man? He will surely reprove you if you secretly show partiality. Will not His majesty terrify you, and the dread of Him fall on you?" (13:7–11)

It almost feels like Job's friends were aliens from another world where there is no evil, describing place that doesn't exist. But we know what the world is like. The place we live in is cruel and quite different from what Job's three friends make it to be. Solomon described in painful detail the poisonous effects on the lives of those who inhabit this earth:

> "Because the sentence against an evil deed is not executed quickly, therefore the hearts of the sons of men among them are given fully to do evil." (Eccl. 8:11)

> "I have seen everything during my lifetime of futility; there is a righteous man who perishes in his righteousness and there is a wicked man who prolongs his life in his wickedness." (Eccl. 7:15)

> "There is futility which is done on the earth, that is, there are righteous men to whom it happens according to the deeds of the wicked." (Eccl. 8:14)

Solomon lived in the world of injustice. This is the world you and I know, and Job saw it the same way. That is why he sternly rebuked his friends after listening to their fantasies. And he told them about the world he lived in. In relating his point of view, Job rightly put God behind everything that happens around us. Every iniquity that happens in the world occurs with God's permission. Has anything changed since ancient times?

"The earth is given into the hand of the wicked; He covers the faces of its judges. If it is not He, then who is it?" (Job 9:24)

"The tents of the destroyers prosper, and those who provoke God are secure, whom God brings into their power. But now ask the beasts, and let them teach you; and the birds of the heavens, and let them tell you. Or speak to the earth, and let it teach you; and let the fish of the sea declare to you. Who among all these does not know that the hand of the Lord has done this." (12:6–9)

"Why do the wicked still live, continue on, also become very powerful? Their descendants are established with them in their sight, and their offspring before their eyes, their houses are safe from fear, and the rod of God is not on them." (21:7–9)

"They send forth their little ones like the flock, and their children skip about. They sing to the timbrel and harp and rejoice at the sound of the flute. They spend their days in prosperity, and suddenly they go down to Sheol. They say to God, 'Depart from us! We do not even desire the knowledge of Your ways. Who is the Almighty, that we should serve Him, and what would we gain if we entreat Him?'" (21:11–15)

"One dies in his full strength, being wholly at ease and satisfied; his sides are filled out with fat, and the marrow of his bones is moist, while another dies with a bitter soul, never even tasting anything good." (21:23–25)

"Have you not asked wayfaring men, and do you not recognize their witness? For the wicked is reserved for the day of calamity; they will be led forth at the day of fury. Who will confront him with his actions, and who will repay him for what he has done? While he is carried to the grave, men will keep watch over his tomb. The clods of the valley will gently cover him; moreover, all men will follow after him, while countless ones go before him. How then will you vainly comfort me, for your answers remain full of falsehood?" (21:29–34)

Let me ask this: didn't he notice before that the world was full of injustice? Didn't he see other godly people suffer? Of course, he saw it, as he himself confirms in the above verses. He must have often raised his eyes to the heavens in total bewilderment as he saw good people suffer from evil. And, of course, this brought up a lot of questions in him. Those were appalling questions that made him feel uneasy. They opened up the possibility of God being uncontrollable and unpredictable. Maybe Job believed that people's misfortunes were the result of their insufficient godliness. He may have thought, "Well, they may have their troubles, but I will try to do better, and my righteousness will be my stronghold. I am well protected, and I my life is predictable" (see 29:18). While he was thriving, he had no pressing need to diligently seek an answer to the question of the world's injustice. But now that the trouble was here (and of a most horrific kind), it was time to include in his theology all of those lifelong observations. It was time to make sure that all his hunches and intuitions about God's uncontrollability were actually true. He realized that all his attempts to protect himself from the unpleasant surprises of life had failed. After spending years and years heavily investing in the heavenly bank, he found himself going bankrupt—at least, that's what he thought. "My days are past, my plans are torn apart, even the wishes of my heart" (17:11).

But let's go back to Job's friends. What prompted them to lie and distort reality? What was the driving force behind it? The answer is obvious—fear! Job saw right through their fear, after the very first speech of Eliphaz, "Indeed, you have now become such, you see a terror and are afraid" (6:21). As we have already mentioned, they saw a threat to their beliefs in Job's tragedy. Their worldview would have suffered a serious blow if it turned out that Job had actually done nothing worthy of punishment. They would have been shocked, just like Job was, and would have had to face a very challenging theological dilemma; if it's not punishment, then *what is it?* How should this be understood? Could God have put all the children of an outstandingly righteous man to death *for no reason?* If Job was innocent, then, according to basic human logic, there was only one alternative; the Creator must be unjust. Job's friends were faced with a choice—to admit that Job was innocent and so embrace God's injustice in punishing him, or to declare Job guilty by claiming that all these calamities were well-deserved. In their understanding, there was no other way to reconcile God's justice with such a horrendous suffering in the life of a righteous man. At the very beginning of their interaction, they must have been in a crisis for a while, which was a turning point for their reasoning. They needed to somehow explain away what had happened, to find evidence for the guilt of the one who "used to be righteous in their eyes." And so, once again, they resorted to telling "white lies."

The Third Mistake—Lying About Job
Sitting next to Job in the dust and mourning according to the customs of their time and culture, they were frantically searching for an explanation. They had seen something dreadful and were frightened. What they saw (not for the first time, I believe) could be interpreted as God's unpredictability. And they did not like it. "It can't be," they stubbornly insisted, "there must be an explanation." The option that God could act unjustly was not even considered, and we must give them credit for it. Bildad rhetorically asks, "Does God pervert justice? Or does the Almighty pervert what is right?" (8:3). There must be only one guilty party—Job! So, they had to change their opinion of this righteous man and "convince" themselves that there was another, darker side to Job's life they didn't know about. Most likely, this change had happened even before Job first spoke. Apparently, they did not expect Job to utter anything except the words of repentance and contrition. Such words would have immediately solved all

their conundrums and brought clarity to the situation. So when Job broke the silence, they became very angry because his speeches did not sound like repentance at all.

At first, they spoke as politely as they could, pointing out that whatever happened to Job was sufficient proof of his wickedness in and of itself. They believed their words would bring him to repentance (4:7–9). But this had no effect on Job, and all the subsequent discourses sound more like duels, rather than conversations between best friends. They hurled angry and hurtful words at each other. Job stubbornly insisted on his innocence, and his friends were outraged at such "lies." However, they had no evidence that Job was lying. The only evidence of Job's "guilt" was the tragedy itself. Nothing else! Yet despite everything Job said, they did not believe him and chose the tactics of "defending God" by telling outright lies about their friend. Eliphaz, for example, went as far as rebuking Job for what he could not prove by a single shred of evidence. Without a moment's thought, he simply leveled grievous accusations at his friend:

> "For your guilt teaches your mouth, and you choose the language of the crafty. Your own mouth condemns you, and not I; and your own lips testify against you." (15:5–6)

> "Is it because of your reverence that He reproves you, that He enters into judgment against you? Is not your wickedness great, and your iniquities without end? For you have taken pledges of your brothers without cause, and stripped men naked. To the weary you have given no water to drink, and from the hungry you have withheld bread. But the earth belongs to the mighty man, and the honorable man dwells in it. You have sent widows away empty, and the strength of the orphans has been crushed. Therefore snares surround you, and sudden dread terrifies you." (22:4–10)

Chapter 3. The Miserable Comforters

It turns out Bildad "knew" why all Job's children perished, saying, "If your sons sinned against Him, then He delivered them into the power of their transgression" (8:4). The wise Job guessed the theological dilemma of his so-called friends and rebuked them for their devious way of trying to escape the test of their faith. In doing so, they forgot about the fear of God. This is like what unscrupulous lawyers do when their only goal is to bail their clients out of trouble. "How painful are honest words! But what does your argument prove? Do you intend to reprove my words, when the words of one in despair belong to the wind? You would even cast lots for the orphans and barter over your friend" (6:25–27).

Job must have known their thoughts. He was trying to convince them that he wasn't lying. He pleaded with them to believe in his innocence, "Now please look at me and see if I lie to your face. Desist now, let there be no injustice. Even desist, my righteousness is yet in it. Is there injustice on my tongue? Cannot my palate discern calamities?" (6:28–30). But all was in vain. "Guilty" was the cruel verdict of the three judges. They simply refused to believe that their close friend could be innocent. Job protested, accused God of injustice and his friends of hypocrisy, while they blamed him for secret sins that must have led to such a terrible punishment. Their cause-and-effect theology required that a cause for such consequences be found. In other words, someone had to end up on trial. There were two suspects, Job and God. No one even thought of a third party. No one could even imagine that Job was innocent, God was just, and that none of Job's trials were punishment. Even though they all believed in God's sovereignty and lordship, none of them wished to apply this doctrine to their own lives to such an extreme degree. In their understanding, God could not act so harshly towards a person, unless He had sufficient grounds for it, namely some terrible sin on the part of the person. But they were wrong!

The Fourth Mistake—Depriving Job Of Human Compassion

It was a time of testing for their friendship and the sincerity of their love. Their longtime friend desperately needed compassion from another human being. But the three "friends" got so carried away playing the role of God's advocates that they completely forgot about compassion. Yet this is what Job mostly needed from them: "For the despairing man there should be kindness from his friend; So that he does not forsake the fear of the Almighty" (6:14). "Pity me, pity me, O you my friends, for the hand of God has struck me" (19:21). Deeply disappointed, Job compares them to a dry wadi.[3] They were the only hope for a weary caravan on a desert trail, but they turned out to be dry and empty (6:15–20). This felt like betrayal! Why couldn't they just sympathize with in him in his grief, without all this empty moralizing?! What can we learn by looking at such kind of "love" the three friends showed to the unfortunate sufferer?

First, we should be very cautious when we start speaking about God, so that we do not distort any facts while trying to help a person. Without truth, there will be no freedom or real comfort. Secondly, just listening attentively to someone who is on the verge of despair is sometimes the best medicine and consolation. "Listen carefully to my speech, and let this be your way of consolation" (21:2). People want to be heard and understood in their grief. This is how we were made. It is important for us to have someone nearby who can sympathize with us in our troubles. It is a very useful skill—to be able to patiently listen to a person without feeling a compulsive desire to give him a moralizing lesson at the end. A person should be allowed to pour out their heart, especially if he or she is in pain. Often, this is the best compassion you can offer. After all, when Job first spoke,

---

[3]Wadi is a valley or ravine that is dry except for brief periods during the rainy season.

all his real thoughts, convictions, plans and feelings came to the surface. And for someone who is trying to help, it is the most valuable information.

"I Don't Know"

Now we have seen what Job's friends did, and we know why. But let's also discuss how they should have acted if they had listened to the promptings of their conscience. All they had to do was to throw up their hands and honestly admit that they had no explanation for what was happening. All they should have said was "I don't know," while grieving and weeping with their friend. Isn't that why they came in the first place? True, these three simple words would have thrown them out of their comfortably fabricated world, where everything was calculable and predictable. They would have ended up in the cold night of uncertainty, so dreaded and hated by many people, and they would have come into the company of an uncontrollable God. These three words would have revealed to them a God they did not know, and honestly, didn't even want to know. These three words would have forced them to reconsider their safe theology. They did not want to return home with the realization that what they had seen happen to Job could happen to them the next day, because it turns out there is nothing you can do to hold God back. They really didn't want to enter into the darkness of God's incomprehensibility. They would rather invent a convenient "explanation" than live in fear of unanswered questions.

Do you understand everything God is doing around you? Can you explain everything? To be honest, we must admit that our human minds cannot fully grasp God's ways. God really is beyond human comprehension! After all, how can a sinner with a corrupted mind comprehend all the doctrines? Also, if I'm sinful and God is holy, how can I *like* everything He does? My duty is just to accept it by faith, knowing that whatever God is doing is the right thing. But I don't have to like everything He does. And I don't need absolute clarity. I'll say even more: it's not normal if I claim to like everything God is doing around me, and that everything is crystal clear to me. If I say so, it only means that I am a hypocrite, and I deceive myself by denying the truth—namely, that God is incomprehensible and righteous, and I am limited and sinful! "God thunders with His voice wondrously, doing great things which we cannot comprehend" (37:5). Who is it talking about? Surely, it's talking about us, the limited people. So, let us not be hypocritical, like Job's friends, pretending that we have no difficult questions left. Because we do.

Let me add a few words about justice to follow up on the previous chapter. There are doctrines in Scripture which can confuse and even frighten us. Take, for example, the doctrine of the eternal punishment for sinners. It's the most difficult one for me personally. It's directly opposite to our human idea of justice. Why should a person pay off approximately sixty-seventy years of sinning with eternity in hell? Why not be sentenced to the same amount of time as you have spent sinning in this life? Okay, let it be a hundred or even a thousand years. I can even understand a million years in hell, but not eternity. There's nothing more horrifying than this! I'm terrified to even think of it. But I can't fully grasp eternity in heaven either, not to mention the opposite. From a purely theological point of view, I can explain all the possible reasons for such a severe retaliation.

But that's not what I'm talking about. What I want to say is that I don't *like* the arguments given; they don't align with my understanding of justice. And what do you say about the doctrine of imputing Adam's guilt to the whole human race (Rom. 5:12–14)? Doesn't it bring up questions? It sure does!

Chapter 3. The Miserable Comforters

I doubt there's anybody out there who never got confused about it: "Why should all humanity bear the sin of one man? Why am I bearing the sin of someone who lived thousands of years before me? And I had no choice in the matter—I wasn't the one who reached for the forbidden fruit. Because of Adam, I was born into sin and began a life of sin even before I realized it. I suffer only because I was born into this family. This isn't fair!" Indeed, from the purely human point of view, it isn't.

Another "difficult" doctrine is the doctrine of unconditional election. I don't like it either! And there are many Christians out there who hate it! According to their understanding, a just God should provide everyone with an equal opportunity of entering His Kingdom. But to say that means that we hypocritically reject the unpleasant realities, and so reject the truth of God's Word. The reality is that there ISN'T such a thing as an equal opportunity for salvation. Why distort the reality and go against the conscience? That's exactly what Job's friends did. I plead with you, just look around and do not lie. Someone was born into a Baptist family in Christian America and lived to a very old age and heard the Gospel a thousand times. Another person was born deep in the Amazon jungle, died of malaria when they were eighteen, and never heard the Good News, just like hundreds of generations before them. Does this sound fair? What would you say? Would you take on the role of God's advocate and try to logically bail the poor kid out of this dilemma? You cannot explain this reality without falling into the error of Job's friends; your erroneous premise is that there is such a thing as equality. But there isn't—even in Heaven. So, you will have to lie.

More importantly, Scripture also opposes the idea of equality, so cherished by many Christians. The book of Romans says that a man is no more than a *work of God's hands*, over which the Creator has the absolute power, and that He is not limited by the finite ideas of justice.

> "On the contrary, who are you, O man, who answers back to God? The thing molded will not say to the molder, "Why did you make me like this," will it? Or does not the potter have a right over the clay, to make from the same lump one vessel for honorable use and another for common use?" (Rom. 9:20–21)

Do you see any equality here? Please show me equality in this passage. Do you see an equal opportunity for salvation for everyone? There's no such thing! Most Christians believe in God's sovereignty. But when the apostle Paul, in speaking of unconditional election, puts his rhetorical question, "Does not the potter have a right over the clay?" Thousands of pots, who allegedly believe in His sovereignty, reply to my utmost dismay, "No, He is not. Hands off, Potter! Long live justice! We will choose what kind of pots we are going to be!" Forgive me, but this sounds more like some kind of Christian communism.

Let me say again, I do not like the doctrine of election, and some other doctrines as well. I wish they didn't exist. However, if there's a clearly stated scriptural truth, then I will embrace it by faith, without regard to my feelings. I do not want to go against my conscience by inventing a comfortable God for myself. Undoubtedly, from a purely human point of view, many of God's actions may seem unfair. Many of us are still in bondage to the same fear that struck Job's friends—that God cannot be controlled and manipulated. This fear often leads to hypocrisy. A lot of people won't admit this fear even to themselves, let alone publicly confess it! Do you sometimes see yourself in Eliphaz, Bildad, and Zophar, who rushed to defend God's "justice" by lying? If so, then it's probably a good time for you to come to grips with what you have long feared. I realize that the God presented in this book may seem scary, to put it mildly. But is it still better than to try to bury our heads in the sand. We can bravely face these difficult questions. It is wiser to recognize that the Creator of the Universe is not going to fit into the mold of our *safe* theology. It is much wiser to allow Him to reveal to us the right theology through His Word, regardless of what we like or dislike. Unfortunately, we often deny what we see in the Word of God, because it doesn't fit our human standards and concepts, and simply because we DO NOT LIKE IT! But then, wouldn't it fall under the category of "They will accumulate . . . teachers in accordance to their own desires" (2 Tim. 4:3)?

We have a tendency to open our minds only to something that does not cause any fear or confusion. But this is a carnal approach! At such times our "old self" is warring against us by filtering the truths of Scripture. When we need to practice humility or trust in the Lord by accepting certain clearly expressed doctrines, the flesh will kick and scream and offer alternative "all-encompassing" interpretations. In these interpretations, there will be ready answers to all the complex questions, no matter if these answers contradict the Scriptures or not. The main thing is that they will give you a picture of a knowable, predictable and, most importantly, just God who fits our human understanding. Don't buy into the lie. It is absolutely normal to worship God while staying in the darkness of uncertainty, to communicate with Him without understanding everything that's going on! This is a mark of humility, a sign of a healthy relationship between a limited creature and the incomprehensible Creator. This is a relationship that's built on faith!

As for me, I choose to believe in the justice of God without looking for ridiculous explanations, even if they proceed from the best of motives. I feel safer in the darkness of God's uncertainty than in the light of human groundless logic. In this darkness I am standing on a solid foundation of the Word of God which gives me peace: "Shall not the Judge of all the earth deal justly?" (Gen. 18:25). I feel safer because I am holding the hand of the One who is not capable of cruelty. I am at peace without any tangible evidence.

How about you? As was mentioned in the previous chapter, the very fact that God calls Himself just should be enough to stop doubting it and seeking exhaustive answers. If God says that eternal punishment in the Lake of Fire is just, then it is just. If God imputes the sin of Adam to all humankind, then it must be so. If God wishes to choose someone for salvation, then it is not contrary to His holiness. There's much I don't understand, but I choose to trust! No one knows all of the answers to complex life questions. It is not always possible to explain why this or that happened. In such situations, you just need to admit it to yourself and instill it in someone who may be expecting an explanation from you. Often pastors and ministers think it their duty to have all the answers just because that's what people expect from them. After all, it's their job, isn't it? But let's be honest, God does not give them any special revelations. They can only know what is revealed in the Scriptures.

So, let's not imitate Job's friends, who refused to accept the mysterious and the incomprehensible, and came up with their own silly interpretations. When you don't know, simply say: "I don't know." Nothing more. We should say it more often. "I don't know." It's our pride that gets in the way of saying these three words: "I don't know!" But then, is it really helping anybody when we keep blathering instead of honestly admitting "I DON'T KNOW"?

> *But you smear with lies;*
> *you are all worthless physicians.*
> *O that you would be completely silent,*
> *and that it would become your wisdom!*
> *(Job 13:4–5)*

> *God thunders with His voice wondrously,*
> *doing great things which we cannot comprehend.*
> *(Job 37:5)*

4

THE FORGOTTEN CHARACTER

Job's wife is the only character in this ancient story whose name is not mentioned. What do we know about her? Very little. Yet what is recorded is quite enough to see her unique role in the unfolding of this universal drama. Isn't it interesting that Satan let her live? Why on earth would someone who was a "murderer from the beginning," a being with no inherent goodness whatsoever, grant someone life when had every chance to take it away? This can only indicate one thing: Job's wife was of much better use for Satan alive and at her husband's side. Satan's "kindness" to her proceeded from the fiendish scenario, according to which she was to strike a staggering blow at the confidence of the righteous man when the time was ripe. And she played her part wonderfully, "Then his wife said to him, 'Do you still hold fast your integrity? Curse God and die!'" (2:9).

Do you remember Satan's ultimate goal in this story? He himself put it like this—to make Job curse God (1:11). Isn't it sad and scary that he would choose as his immediate instrument someone who was Job's closest companion? Without knowing it, Job's wife became Satan's greatest ally in subverting her husband's faith. The wife of the righteous man, on whom the stamp of God's highest approval was placed, was the one who gave voice to Satan's ultimate purpose in all his dealings with him: "Curse God and die." How insidious! How treacherous! Such insane advice could only be interpreted as follows: either she was calling on the righteous man to curse God and commit suicide, or else she believed that the blasphemy itself would result in God's killing Job. In any case, it was, without a doubt, the worst piece of "wisdom" she ever gave to her husband.

What would prompt her to do such a horrific act? Was it madness which was the result of grief? Indeed, it is understandable that someone would go insane after losing all their children in one day. After all, she had to endure the same hellish torment as Job would, except for the illness. Yet, unlike her husband, she lost her faith. Her spirit crumbled. All love, pity, and the fear of God were gone, even though she had been previously basking in the goodness of God every single day. There was nothing left in her but anger and despair.

"Do You Still Hold Fast to Your Integrity?"

This question, as well as the following sentence, clearly demonstrates her spiritual condition. Basically, she's asking two questions in one: (1) what's the point of keeping integrity if there's no benefit in it? (2) Why live, if everything you've ever lived for has been taken away? Their actual value system was revealed in how each one reacted to the tragedy. I hope I won't come across

Chapter 4. The Forgotten Character

as too harsh or severe in what I am going to say, but let me first elaborate my point.

There was a significant difference between Job and his wife's spiritual condition. It seems to me that she had never had a living faith in her heart at any time. She had no need for the God of Job, whether in times of bliss or in times of trouble. She saw God as her husband's employer who had a profitable business and was helping them along on the road to prosperity. She must have been very religious. It is *religion,* not faith, that teaches a person to negotiate with God—to worship Him when He is good and curse Him when He is bad. Religion's worship is always conditional. So now that they were in trouble, this woman had no more reason to play the role of a pious wife—why would she?

I am sure that Job's piety reflected on his whole family, at least externally. His wife and children knew the difference between good and evil very well, what was pleasing to the Lord and what He despised. It would have been impossible to live with Job, to experience his godliness on a daily basis, and not follow his rules. We could safely say that their marriage revolved around Job's relationship with God. His wife couldn't help but see Job's profound faith in all his actions every day, reaping its fruit in how he treated her, in how he raised their children, cared for the poor, and met the needs of the destitute. Undoubtedly, she had heard him teach the fear of God to the whole family when they were spending time together. She must have seen him pray and offer sacrifices. She *knew better than anyone else* that for him it was for real and not just going through the motions; it was the meaning of his life. Didn't she know that Job had once made a covenant with his eyes (31:1), so now she could enjoy her husband's unshakable fidelity in marriage? Didn't she see how the poor and the destitute were getting protection under his wing (31:16–20)? Of course she did. She knew it all, she saw it all, and if her husband had led a double life or there had been some sin in his past, it would have been a great time to remind him of it. After all, your spouse is the last person who could be deceived about your true character. Her own words "Do you still hold fast your integrity?" are the best testimony to her absolute faith in his character.

However, the most striking testimony to Job's integrity, and proof that Someone up there was very pleased with him, was the constant river of blessings, the untold riches, the almost universal love and respect that poured down from Heaven. The children were all healthy, well-off and had good lives. The future seemed bright and promising. What else could a wife and mother wish for? Only for one thing; to have it last forever. But the bliss ended, abruptly and irrevocably. Her ten children she bore, nursed and raised, to whom she dedicated her youth and all her strength—those children, who would soon bless her old age with grandchildren and great-grandchildren, were now gone, buried in their graves. They were gone forever, never to return. And her husband, the greatest of the sons of the East, was humiliated and crushed. He was sitting on a pile of ashes, rotting alive like some filthy tramp. I don't believe I could adequately express her state of mind at such a time.

Can we empathize with her as fellow human beings and cry together with her? Certainly. Can we justify her apostasy? According to biblical theology—no. In dire situations like this, it is very unwise to let our sinful old self pass judgements about what is happening. In spiritual matters, our flesh is as blind as a mole. From a purely fleshly point of view, one could argue that she had gone through incredible pain, which could have forced her to say crazy things, like suggest that her husband should curse God. It's also possible to justify her by pointing out that it must have been Satan who was putting words in her mouth. In Scripture we see that the devil indeed can pressure people to act in certain ways, and it is especially true of those who do not have saving faith in their hearts. As soon as God allowed Satan to lay his hand on Job, the enemy immediately brought the Sabeans and Chaldeans upon him. So one day, the two tribes raided the numerous herds of this well-known man—possibly, without any plot. Satan made sure that the Sabeans and Chaldeans each left at least one shepherd alive who would then break the terrible news to the patriarch. Others were put to the sword. It is clear that some people do Satan's bidding of their own accord when they aren't filled with the Spirit of God and harden their consciousness, such as Judas Iscariot (John 13:2).

But what about Job's wife? Was she a puppet too, uttering the words of Satan like a mechanical wind-up toy, or was it an expression of her own unbelief? One can only say with certainty that in this case (and in all similar cases as well), both things were true. The reason she became Satan's toy was her own unbelief. She unwittingly served the enemy, precisely because she did not care to please the Lord and grow in her faith. As an intelligent being, Satan knew the condition of her heart and gave her a specific role in these events, which aligned with her spiritual state. In the crucible of pain, her religious heart simply could not and did not wish to prolong the show of external piety. The chaff had to be burned, the iron had to be tempered. This is exactly what happened. And this is the watershed between faith and religion. Both fix their gaze upon the Creator and pray to him while He blesses them. But when he sends hardship and suffering, or when the heavens are silent, religion throws off the mask of piety, and starts cursing and grumbling. Why? Because religion is not interested in God Himself, only in what He can give. This is what happened to Job's wife. We can't even properly say that she rejected God at that moment. It's possible that she never knew Him. All these terrible trials simply revealed what she had always had in her heart—an outward appearance of faith. Our pseudo-faith is rarely seen when life is good. We can deceive ourselves for a long time, thinking that we are believers. In some ways, it's similar to bicycle racing (I say this from personal experience): the first racer, who is ahead of everyone else, takes on the brunt of the wind's resistance, and, consequently, gets tired very quickly. The next one in line gets to rest. The second position allows you to easily maintain any speed you like, even if you're not a good athlete—the position of the leader is so much more difficult. The racer who keeps at the back of the peloton is tempted to think too highly of his own athletic abilities. But as soon as he gets to the front lines and tests himself against the wind, it becomes obvious what he is really capable of.

In the same way, the heart of Job's wife was tested by the trial. For many years she was, so to speak, a "parasite" of her husband's faith. Keeping at the back of the race, she followed just outwardly, hiding from the winds of the relationship with God. If she ever blessed the name of God, it was because God was blessing her. She did not have to exercise her faith, because life was coming easy. She didn't have to strain, because there was always someone else to do all the hard work in the spiritual realm. She could just enjoy her earthly bliss. But then, a mighty gust of wind swept her off her feet, and there was no energy left. There was no strength nor desire left to continue the race. She didn't need the Creator anymore. All she needed was His gifts. Now that the gifts were taken away, she rejected the Giver with contempt.

She didn't even care to understand why the tragedy came. And it's not surprising, since she didn't have her husband's personal relationship with God (Job 12:4), and she probably didn't give much thought to God's actions in the world, His character or nature. It's not surprising if we consider that she was not interested in God as a Person, to whom you can come and pour out your heart, share your thoughts and feelings. Most likely she did nothing of the sort. So when calamity hit and Job was frantically searching for answers, she was just looking on. Does it really matter why it happened, if there's nothing you can do

Chapter 4. The Forgotten Character

to reverse it? Will the answer to the question "why" really help? Their lives are ruined. If she had questions, they must have been very different.

By her very actions she demonstrated that her only concern was the loss she suffered. She focused entirely on the aftermath of the tragedy without any desire to look for causes. Her husband, however, focused on the causes. For Job it was a matter of life and death to figure out God's actions because his whole world revolved around his relationship with God and worshiping Him. For Job it was like getting a slap in the face from a dear friend. How could you not try to figure out what caused such a disgrace? How could you not want to see him face to face? How could you not try to guess the possible reasons? How could you not be confused? Job's behavior was natural—for a *believer*.

Job was like the captain of a ship that was caught up in a storm and totally wrecked by the ruthless waves. After the storm, worn and exhausted, stranded on a half-demolished vessel, he was frantically going through the sea charts, making measurements, checking the compass, running back and forth across the deck, tearing out his hair and desperately trying to understand how he got into such a mess. According to his calculations, he should have passed clear of the storm. His wife, however, is more like the captain's first mate, sitting on what's left of the deck, smoking a pipe and watching the captain go crazy in the midst of the wreckage. She doesn't care whose fault it was. She wasn't the one to set the course, she didn't peer anxiously into the horizon or wait for the right wind. She didn't try to do any of these things. And why would she? There is someone else on board who can do it so much better. She enjoyed her time on the ship, being well-fed, safe in all her voyages, and most importantly, having a very fortunate captain, who was able to navigate successfully through all the storms. That was all she wanted. Now, as she watched her captain, she tried to remember if there was ever a sea

69

captain who had fallen into a similar plight, and she answered, "Probably not." A fortunate man was transformed into a loser before her very eyes. She was deeply disappointed and could only think of how unfair this situation was. It was high time she found another job, and so, out of the sheer kindness of her heart, she gave her captain a piece of advice—go drown yourself.

Job's wife didn't care a bit whether God was just or unjust under the circumstances. She didn't care whether it was punishment, an accident, or something else. She didn't care whether there were some eternal mysteries involved or theological riddles to solve. Even if God was trying to communicate something through these events, what did it matter? Nothing could be changed. It was all over. She was not only bored but also offended by the very idea of communicating with God about it, asking Him questions and giving her mental energy to analyzing the situation.

Quid Pro Quo

Religion's worship is always conditional. To receive honor and glory from a person with a religious heart, God must act in a certain way—meeting certain conditions. A religious man comes to God in the same way he would come to a marketplace. He wants to buy something, and of course, he has something to pay for it. The seller has something the buyer wants, and vice versa. This is a mutually beneficial transaction. Now imagine a buyer paying for the goods, and the seller not delivering them. Well, this is against the law, it's a crime. "What's happening? I just paid you," shouts the deceived party indignantly. "Give me my potatoes!" And if the buyer doesn't get his potatoes, he will never do business with this seller for the rest of his life, carefully avoiding being fooled by other unscrupulous vendors. There are many who try to worship God in the same way. They offer him their self-righteous, lifeless, formal, external "worship" by listening to sermons, participating in liturgies, paying their tithes, singing their hymns and bowing their heads in prayer. In and of themselves, these religious acts do not have much value to them and do not bring any joy. They are nothing but a payment for what they really value—the earthly blessings.

When God refused to "deliver" and stripped them of everything they had, Job's wife reacted in the same way as she would have reacted in the marketplace. For her, there was little difference between the two situations. If there ever was a prayer in her life, it was now pointless. It didn't deliver. Now that God didn't honor His part of the "deal," there was no need to honor Him. There was nothing attractive about worship anymore—it didn't yield anything of value. Job's wife was totally sincere when she suggested that her husband should curse God. Why worship someone who broke their part of the bargain? Like a deceived buyer, she shouted, "I will have nothing to do with this swindler anymore! I don't need a God like this. And I don't understand why you would. You should pay him back in some way!"

Not only did this poor woman reject God, she also became a stumbling block in her husband's path. She didn't want to draw close to Him and share their common grief so they could endure it together. No, Job was truly alone—she, who was supposed to be his helper and supporter, turned out to be a source of additional pain. How would it feel to hear such things from your own wife? It must have been excruciating to have his closest life companion spit out a cynical comment, "Every man for himself!" instead of lending a helping hand. In this way she communicated to Job that she had nothing of value remaining in this world. God was not on her list of life priorities—neither was Job. She had nothing left here that was worth living for. When the earthly blessing that gave meaning to her life ceased, worship became pointless. In a nutshell, she only saw her children's wellbeing and prosperity as worthy goals, not wishing to worship God in the darkness of uncertainty. She viewed God as the power that existed only to provide and maintain her earthly bliss and she was ready to pay for it with her "worship." Now that God failed to give it and the happiness she hoped for was gone, she cursed Him and trampled Him in the mud, like an amulet that didn't protect her from misfortune. It was good for nothing. This is how she saw the goal of worship.

In Job's list of life priorities, God was number one. God was his biggest treasure in life, and so, when everything else was lost, his treasure was still there. And although Job was in deep sorrow and yearned for death, for him life was not finished as long as God was there keeping him alive. And while he was still alive, he kept worshiping the Creator, because for him nothing had changed. "Then Job arose and tore his robe and shaved his head, and he fell to the ground and worshiped" (1:20). The meaning of his life was not lost, even though it suffered a staggering blow. Job answered his wife as someone in whom God's heart was fully confident:

> "But he said to her, 'You speak as one of the foolish women speaks. Shall we indeed accept good from God and not accept adversity?' In all this Job did not sin with his lips." (2:10)

This man's impeccable character was further demonstrated in that he was able to offer his wife some feasible pastoral help while at the peak of his own suffering. At that moment, she needed the sobering truth more than being comforted. True, her agony was real. There was hardly anyone in the recorded history of the world who had suffered what she had suffered.

It is impossible to imagine the feelings of a mother who had lost all of her ten grown children in one day. A modern psychologist might say, "How can we expect a person be psychologically stable in times like these?" Maybe it wasn't a good idea to preach

Chapter 4. The Forgotten Character

to a woman in such a state of mind? Perhaps she wasn't thinking clearly and was just venting her emotions without any bad intentions. However, let us note that God would not have recorded the only remark of a nameless character unless her words should be taken very seriously. She was not a deluded person who had lost her mind as a result of suffering. What she said was a clear temptation to Job, and her "theology" was the worldview of an unbeliever, disillusioned with God. Her irrational advice was stated in a rational manner; she gave it deliberately, fully aware of what she was saying. That's why Job did not dismiss her remark, but answered with a rebuke, "You speak as one of the foolish women speaks . . ." Notice that he did not call her foolish; he just pointed out that she was acting foolishly. He saw right through the solution she offered. She believed it was pointless to continue clinging to piety and pleasing God under such circumstances: "Curse God and die." The extreme degree of pride of someone who is suffering without the fear of God is revealed in their intentional rejection of God when everything they truly valued in life is taken away. Unable to change the situation, they will, in their powerless rage, try to take revenge on the Creator. But in the end, they will only hurt themselves and their loved ones. This a senseless act of rebellion which arises from the depraved and unconverted heart, rooted in self-will and idolatry.

Are we only to be with God when He is "good"? Is there really a good enough reason for a creature to reject the Creator and, more importantly, does this bring us relief?! There is nothing reasonable or comforting in our rejection of God. This is not a way out, but a downward spiral into darkness and despair. If you throw God out of your life, after you have lost everything else, what will you have in the end? Isn't it sheer foolishness? Job was right—it was foolishness. Knowing this, he tried to reason with his wife. She may have failed him, but he did not repay her in the same coin, continuing to take care of her spiritually.

Obviously, his response was not a desperate attempt to cling to life, on the contrary! Actually, he wished he could die (9:21). Yet, this was his idea of true worship. This is how he expressed the essence of being truly devoted to God. True devotion is unconditional! It leaves no room for negotiations, conditions, demands or complaints. It doesn't connect faith to blessings. Job said something to this effect, "I will worship God no matter what. No circumstance is a good enough reason for me to stop worshiping." His words harmonize well with the words of Habakkuk,

> "Though the fig tree should not blossom
> and there be no fruit on the vines,
> Though the yield of the olive should fail
> and the fields produce no food,
> Though the flock should be cut off from the fold
> and there be no cattle in the stalls,
> yet I will exult in the Lord,
> I will rejoice in the God of my salvation." (Hab. 3:17–18)

So the sin of Job's wife must have been great indeed. By uttering just a few words (recorded for our sake), she made the most awful statement in all of Scripture. Maybe this is why God didn't allow us to know her name. For she encouraged her husband to curse the One who is the meaning of life. The whole earth, with all its blessings and joys, is nothing compared to one minute in the presence of the Creator. Isn't all we have in life rubbish compared to him (Phil. 3:8)?

The worst crime that a creature can commit is to refuse to know the One in whose image he was made. He just goes on with his life, ignoring God, or sometimes angrily rejecting Him. He will, of course, accept God's blessings, but without giving thanks, taking them for granted. All he does is consume as much as possible, and if something bad happens, he throws his cynical and spiteful jabs up against Heaven: "What was your God thinking?" This question reveals the shocking truth about the disgustingly ungrateful human heart and the impudent consumerism of God's creatures in relation to their Creator. While God blesses them, they will at best ignore Him, just like they ignore a doormat, living as they please. But as soon as trouble comes their way, they will suddenly lash out and label God as unjust and cruel, blaming Him for not being faithful. They are convinced that He should have protected the one whose very lifestyle disowned Him and cursed His holy name through ungodliness. A legitimate question arises: What is the source of such expectations? Why do those who don't bother to open their mouths in prayer for decades, suddenly pounce on God with bitter resentment, acting as if they had a friend who betrayed their trust? There's a lot to be said on this topic, but the main reason for such an inconsistency is actually quite simple—unbelief. For the unbeliever, God is *always* to blame, regardless of what He does. He is either guilty for being too demanding—after all, faith is a private matter (for most people, even though it actually means, "God, just leave me alone")—or for injustice because He doesn't seem to care about my life not going so well compared to other people. God will hear them say all kinds of things, except the words of gratitude and appreciation.

"Shall We Indeed Accept Good From God And Not Accept Adversity?"

And what about believers? Do we know how to appreciate the goodness of God, poured down on us in so many ways? The most vivid expression of His grace is, of course, the cross. Without it, there is no salvation, yet His goodness is much more than that. It's revealed in a glass of water, in a piece of bread, in a ray of sunshine, in the fragrance of spring, in the warmth of your bed, in the comfort of your home, in the eyes of someone you love and in millions upon millions of other blessings that come to us on this accursed planet. God gives ample evidence of His goodness every day, but not everyone is able to see and appreciate it. Sadly, we often appreciate something only after it is lost. This is how our sinful human nature manifests itself. If you cannot appreciate a cup of tea, your joy will be short-lived even if the next day the Lord gives you a house! Joy and gratitude do not depend on the size of the gift, but on the ability to appreciate it and be grateful. Don't think that only expensive and desirable gifts can make you truly happy. If you cannot be happy with what you have, you will never be happy with all of the things you desire. Contentment is not the result of having a certain measure of wealth, but a state of mind in which you know how to be pleased and grateful.

We should be thankful always, for everything. For a Christian, gratitude is a daily practice. Obviously, it's much easier to be grateful when you have finally received what you have always been dreaming of. But non-believers are also capable of this. It doesn't require much effort. But how often do you thank God when He has taken away something you value? The most natural thing to do under such circumstances is to grumble. Very few people think of an alternative; to thank God for the time allowed to enjoy this blessing, sincerely and wholeheartedly. Why not glorify Him for the joy received, even though it has passed? After all, it was a gift in the first place, which didn't have to come at all! God does not owe us anything, whether in the past or in the future. It's all sheer grace. It's all His goodness! So, if at some point He should decide to take it away, it's important to remember that we never owned it in the first place.

There's only one reason why a person is not able to let go of something, humbly accepting the loss. The reason is that they didn't receive it in the proper way! They received it as their sole possession, not as a steward or a manager. When we receive a blessing from God, we tend to forget our position before God or do not fully understand who we are. We do not see that as stewards, we just manage someone else's estate temporarily. That's why we often view blessings from the Lord as if they were ours to possess, believing ourselves to be entitled to them for forever. We are not able to just enjoy God's blessings with gratitude, without clinging to them. We send our roots deep down into our earthly joys, and we live, breathe and have our being in them. We keep them close to heart and go crazy when something threatens to take them away. This is called idolatry. Essentially, idolatry is misusing God's gifts, meaning to use it in the wrong way. We were not given spouses, careers, money, comforts or other good things to substitute God as objects of worship. These are God's generous gifts which are supposed to give us joy, yet none of these things can replace the Lord. Nothing can take His place!

In our relationship with God, we do not have the right to accept or reject things selectively. As Job noted, "Shall we indeed accept good from God and not accept adversity?" (Job 2:10). To have faith means, in some sense, to refocus from what was given or taken away to the One who gives or takes away. The most important thing in our lives is not life itself, but the One who gives it. Unlike his wife, Job knew this very well. His life wasn't over even after it was ruined. This doesn't mean that it was easy for him to accept the loss—whether it was hard or easy is actually beside the point. The main thing is that he saw it as the will of the Lord. We must train ourselves to fulfill God's moral will and accept His sovereign will, whether we like it or not. Job, like his wife, did not like this idea at all. And who would? Yet, Job lived according to the principle, *"Thy* will be done." That's why he accepted the trials regardless of the terrible suffering he was going through. He did what was right, rejecting his natural human tendencies—if we can put it this way. His faith ran through the gauntlet of his own excruciating and extremely negative thoughts and feelings which hurt like lashes on his back. Job entertained some of these thoughts and feelings for a long time, as we have already mentioned above. But his faith prevailed in the struggle. It stood firm to the end!

I know from my own experience that my mind would at times wage war against my faith, mercilessly beating it up with challenging questions that have no answers. For all I know, Satan may be part of that: "In addition to all, taking up the shield of faith with which you will be able to extinguish all the flaming arrows of the evil one" (Eph. 6:16). Those who are armed with living faith always come out victorious, because their faith is anchored in the mighty power of the Spirit who is indwelling every Christian. "Greater is He who is in you than he who is in the world" (1 John 4:4). Living faith never fails. Our weary minds can be defeated in this long battle—sometimes they just don't know what to make of the ringing silence in response to our difficult and terrifying questions. Our broken hearts seem to fall into the bottomless pit of utter despair. But contrary to all the laws of common sense, our faith will keep breathing and will, like the last standing soldier, bravely defend the Holy of Holies of the believing heart—the confidence that God is good.

As for Job's wife, she did not withstand the onslaught of the trials. Giving way to her own godless thoughts and feelings, she was defeated, since she had no shield to protect herself with. As I mentioned before, it's very unlikely that she had any faith to begin with. The fiery arrows of Satan's temptation pierced right through her heart, and the words of hatred broke out of the bleeding wound. Job, however, withstood the vile attack of the one who was his closest companion in life. Having rebuked his spouse, he simultaneously gave a fitting rebuff to Satan, who obviously had lost the wager. We do not know what happened to this woman. Throughout the book, she is only mentioned one other time, and not in the best light (Job 19:17). We don't know if she was the mother of Job's other children. We don't know if she repented of her godlessness or not, but I do believe it is useful for us to carefully examine her case and draw the valuable life lessons that lie within.

The fear of the Lord is a fountain of life,
that one may avoid the snares of death.
(Prov. 14:27)

5
HOPE

The theme of hope runs throughout the entire book of Job. Isn't it much easier to endure sufferings when you know that you will soon be comforted? Hope is a wonderful and beautiful thing. Every one of us has his own desires and dreams. We seem to automatically start our day in hope that it will bring us something pleasant. When we are hungry, we look forward to having lunch. A separation is more bearable when we know we will see the other person again. We long to get home after a hard day's work, and we joyfully watch the clock tick the last few minutes of our shifts. We all have our pleasures in life, whether big or small, and they help us get through the day. We look forward to all sorts of things: meeting someone we've long missed, a weekend, a new purchase, a sporting event, visiting with friends, a picnic, a journey, etc. All these things brighten our daily routines by giving us something to hope for. We seem to always peek into the future with some degree of anticipation. Even if there's nothing specific to hope for, we still expect the best. It is our nature; hope gives us the motivation to go on.

Every person inevitably puts his hope in something or someone. Even those who commit suicide are not entirely without hope—they hope to be relieved of their suffering by killing themselves. Therefore, they are taking their lives *in hope*. Such a person sees death as a desirable escape from something which is worse than death. Therefore, from a purely logical standpoint, when a person takes his life, he is not in an entirely hopeless situation; he sort of has a way out. We, who are alive, have no idea what it feels like to have no hope at all. No one while living has ever experienced the full deprivation of hope. There is only one place where hope is totally absent; it is Hell.

Let's think about Hell for a while. "Abandon all hope, ye who enter here," runs Dante's famous observation. The poet succinctly captured the most terrible characteristic of Hell—its eternity. Hell is a scary place not so much because of its tortures, but because these tortures never end. Any suffering can be endured when you know it's temporary. How much worse it is to have a punishment that lasts forever! Every true Christian has thought about this place where we all would have ended up had it not been for the mercy of God in Jesus Christ. As for me, I am quite terrified at the very idea of Hell. According to the Scriptures, the two main events that await all those who are imprisoned in Hell at this time are: the great white throne judgement and the judgement of lake of fire (Rev. 20:12–15). There is very little hope in these events. As the saying goes— out of the frying pan and into the fire. It's hard for me even to imagine what it must be like to live with the full knowledge that there is nothing good to hope for. What is it like to suffer in the absolute assurance that there will *never* be any relief? How does a person feel when his or her life has been deprived of the very concept of hope, when their only foreseeable future is the dark gloom of eternal damnation? How can you resign to the idea that there will be no end to pain? All of the horror movies that our human imagination has ever come up with are but naive childish fantasies compared to the horrors of the underworld. And this horror was invented by God! A loving God prepared Hell for His enemies (Matt. 25:41). Paradoxically, Hell is probably the best testimony to God's fierce holiness and His ardent hatred of sin.

I'm convinced that for inhabitants of the underworld, death (as cessation of existence) is the most cherished dream and the deepest desire of their hearts. For their situation, there's no better escape than to be annihilated (stop thinking, feeling, remembering, etc.). Why live when all your thoughts, feelings and memories bring nothing but anguish?! It's no longer living but a wretched and meaningless existence, deprived of all purpose and hope. Maybe that's why the Bible calls this state "eternal death." Thanks be to Jesus Christ—I will never experience these feelings.

Wouldn't you agree that in light of all we know about Hell, our daily problems seem very insignificant? They say that the value of everything is known through comparison. We will certainly see our problems in a different light when we compare them with the weight of future glory which will be revealed in Jesus Christ (2 Cor. 4:17). There is enough pain on this earth—at times we all feel a temptation to fall into despair. Even strong believers may for a season forget about their great hope and succumb to the overwhelming feelings of despondency. No doubt, a person's reaction to suffering is an indicator of how he understands hope. Job is a perfect example of this. Let us examine his thoughts and words, and how they were influenced by hope:

"What is my strength, that I should wait? And what is my end, that I should endure?" (Job 6:11). Later he cries, "Where now is my hope? And who regards my hope? Will it go down with me to Sheol? Shall we together go down into the dust?" (17:15–16).

These statements clearly indicate a state of mind in which a person has nothing left on this earth that would be worth living for, nothing that would motivate him to go on. All the anchors of your lifeboat have been torn loose by the ferocious winds of life, and your little vessel is thrown about in the midst of the raging abyss. In Job, we see how despair shifts our focus from God to grief, filling up our whole existence with the all-encompassing darkness and pushing God and all hope out of our consciousness. Instead of looking forward to the bright and joyful future, we fix our gaze upon the past (which is gone and lost) and on the pain of the present moment: "And Job again took up his discourse and said, 'Oh that I were as in months gone by, as in the days when God watched over me'" (29:1–2).[1] "But now those younger than I mock me, whose fathers I disdained to put with the dogs of my flock" (30:1).[2] Even if such a person thinks about the future, he will see it as hopeless and dismal. Job, for example, concluded that his days on earth were numbered, "My days are swifter than a weaver's shuttle, and come to an end without hope. Remember that my life is but breath; my eye will not again see good" (7:6–7). Although later events proved him wrong, at that particular moment Job truly believed that his life was over, and that, according to his own scenario, there was nothing left in this world to look forward to: ". . . my eye will not again see good." Now that all his hopes for the earthly bliss were dashed, he gave himself the permission to do something he had never done before—grumble. It was a hasty decision, but it became the driving force behind all his

---

[1] See also Chapter 29.
[2] See also Chapter 30.

complaints. "Therefore I will not restrain my mouth; I will speak in the anguish of my spirit, I will complain in the bitterness of my soul" (7:11).

Expectations

Grumbling is inescapable when our focus is shifted from God to our problems, pain or losses. There comes a time when we, like Job, will face a choice: should we keep our mouths shut or should we open them to complain? Let's see how grumbling is connected to our expectations in relation to God.

We always have our own ideas and plans for any given situation. We bring this plan to God in prayer and ask him to carry it out for us. However, should something go wrong, we feel a strong temptation to complain. Imagine that you have been diligently asking for something, fasting and even kneeling down with the whole church to pray for the situation, yet God is systematically and ruthlessly thwarting your plans and bringing about your worst fears. This is exactly what happened to Job (3:25). Theology is always integrated with expectations. Expectations are akin to hope; they are, in essence, a person's response to God's promises. We cannot really say that Job had any specific promises from God concerning his earthly life. More likely, his expectations were based on a general understanding of the character of God that he worshiped. According to his own understanding, God could not have withheld blessings from him because of his piety. Job's expectations were directly related to his righteousness.

> "For when the ear heard, it called me blessed, and when the eye saw, it gave witness of me, because I delivered the poor who cried for help, and the orphan who had no helper. The

blessing of the one ready to perish came upon me, and I made the widow's heart sing for joy. I put on righteousness, and it clothed me; my justice was like a robe and a turban. I was eyes to the blind and feet to the lame. I was a father to the needy, and I investigated the case which I did not know. I broke the jaws of the wicked and snatched the prey from his teeth. Then I thought, 'I shall die in my nest, and I shall multiply my days as the sand. My root is spread out to the waters, and dew lies all night on my branch. My glory is ever new with me, and my bow is renewed in my hand." (29:11–20)

We see the same logic developing in the next chapter, "Have I not wept for the one whose life is hard? Was not my soul grieved for the needy? When I expected good, then evil came; when I waited for light, then darkness came" (30:25–26). We see here that Job's mind was connecting piety to blessings. Indeed, how can you expect a just God to punish someone who was leading such a God-centered life? Expectations can be a dangerous thing if they rest on a wrong foundation. People often get disappointed in God the Almighty—and for various reasons: He failed to lead to repentance someone the whole church was praying for many years to be saved, or He failed to heal, protect and bless. Are you one of them? If you expected one thing, but got something entirely different, how did you explain it to yourself? Did you blame God for not coming through for you, or did you review your expectations? I hope the latter; my hope is that you didn't put God on the stand.

If you are like me, you must have also tried or are still trying to guess how the Lord will act in a given situation. But you know what? It's no use trying to predict, much less to plan for certain things to happen just based on your past experiences of success or failures. God's ways are not our ways. He will decide who needs

Chapter 5. Hope

to learn a lesson—regardless of what our human logic predicts. But why would a loving God hurt us? Does He delight in causing us pain? Of course not. But he is pursuing totally different goals than our flesh is. We may be looking for safety on Earth, but he is teaching us godliness by taking away our safety. We may be looking for control, but He is showing us how to trust by putting us through desperate circumstances every once in a while. We may be seeking pleasures apart from him, but He is teaching us to delight in Him by limiting our access to earthly pleasures. We may be seeking our own glory, but He is teaching us to glorify Him only. We may be looking to provide for our earthly lives, but He is preparing us for the life to come. In a nutshell, while we may be building our own paradise on earth, He is reminding us to seek His face, find our joy in Him and worship him. He has to deny us certain things so He can reach His goals (Jam. 4:3). That's why at times we all feel disappointed in God. Our complaints about His actions are similar to a child's reaction to his parents' not giving him the ice cream that he asked for, but a bowl of oatmeal he didn't want. Aren't your children upset when you send them to bed every night? Don't they want to sleep in when you try to wake them up for school? Do they always do everything you tell them the first time? I don't think so. They always have a strong opinion about *what* they need, *when* they need it, and *how much* of it they need. But because you pursue their highest good, you do not always comply with their desires, but disappoint them!

In the same way God "disappoints" us by pursuing His own goals with us and by leaving some of our legitimate desires unfulfilled because too often they revolve around our earthly existence. Instead, He fosters other desires in our hearts which have to do with our spiritual character formation. Our flesh, of course, does not like it. It will never humbly accept God's script for your life. It will resist, yell, wriggle and kick. So, the process of our sanctification, in which we are personally involved, *must* include disappointments. There is no other way for us to be purified of sin. In the final analysis, we must choose between displeasing either the Spirit of God or our flesh. It's impossible to please them both, because, as we have already said above, they pursue different goals.

To set the right goal, you must first reject the wrong one, but since people are stubborn by nature, it may take them quite some time. Unfortunately, many Christians take a lifetime to do it! When I hear of visitors to churches who are chased away from their seats by some older lady who had "claimed" the spot for herself, I can't help but feel devastated and hopeless; some people seem to need more than a lifetime to learn the basics.

Let me share with you my own personal story of being disappointed in God. Since I was young, I had my own script for how I would be living my life. According to my scenario, I would have everything I ever wanted and just the way I wanted it. When I came to faith at twenty, I slightly revised my plan so as to accommodate my new worldview. This new "Christian" version was perfect in every way, because now it had a new and key element in it—God. I generously allowed God to join my life as my personal bodyguard and financial planner. My whole Christian philosophy at that time was as follows: "God buys me gas, and I drive." I was overjoyed at the thought that now I had the Almighty on my side, and that my chances of success in life were one hundred percent. Finally, I would have everything I ever wanted out of life! Totally delighted, I presented my magnificent life plan to God for approval, anticipating a shower of blessings to come down from Heaven. Can you guess what God did? Nothing! Up to this day my perfect script is gathering dust on the shelves of God's office. Instead, He gave me a new script, which I hated the moment I saw it. I began to grumble and throw tantrums. Numerous times, as I was lamenting my unfulfilled desires and broken dreams,

Chapter 5. Hope

I was writhing in pain and wallowing in helpless rage, telling God literally the following: "Ah, if only I could hurt you like you hurt me, I would certainly do it!" The self-proclaimed god of my imagination was slowly dying under the pressures of the liberating truth of the Word of God while I was hurling insults at the one true God. Instead of the longed for ice cream, I was invariably getting the disdained oatmeal.

It was not until I heard the Gospel call to "deny yourself" that I finally woke up. "For whoever wishes to save his life will lose it; but whoever loses his life for My sake will find it" (Matt. 16:24–25). Suddenly I realized that all these years I had been doing just the opposite—carefully guarding and saving my own life! I was clinging to it with all my strength while bemoaning my precious dreams and moping over my thwarted plans and unwanted trials. In the meantime, Jesus was patiently unclenching my fingers, which I had put around my own throat, and leading me towards freedom out of the prison of dire egocentrism. Oh, how I was kicking and screaming! I insisted on my "rights," grumbling and pouting! Does it sound funny to you? Seems pretty tragic to me. Dying to myself and denying my own plans took me several long years, and even now I still have to fight my flesh every day.

As I reflect on all those years, I can't help thinking of a scene from the classic Soviet film "They Fought for Their Country." Private Zvyagintsev is badly injured in a mine explosion. He is on the table in the medical unit, waiting for the surgeon to extract some fragments of the mine out of his back. Naturally, there is no anesthesia except for alcohol. Zvyagintsev is writhing, howling, grinding his teeth, and cursing the surgeon with all his might. He could have probably crawled away from the place of his torture, but he stays there, realizing that the surgeon is doing a good thing. The only alternative is death. In much the same way, our Heavenly Surgeon is extracting out of our souls whatever is hurtful and dangerous for us, so we can live a full life. Although many of us allow Him to do His work by staying on the table, we still hurl insults at Him in anger instead of thanking Him for saving us from death.

Grumbling

Grumbling is not just about saying words. This is a certain attitude that reflects the state of our hearts. There are many ways to grumble—words are just one way to do it. We can grumble with our face, eyes, or gestures. We can grumble without realizing that we are grumbling. Our conscience is more attuned to the "obvious" sins, like those expressed in words or actions, therefore we often overlook sins that do not manifest themselves in the usual way. In other words, you can grumble *without saying anything*. But even if we grumble silently, we are still grumbling. God hears what's going on in our hearts. To detect the secret attitude of your heart, use the method of exclusion, which works perfectly. If we do not continually thank God for things in our lives, we inevitably grumble. There is no middle ground. Either we wholeheartedly say, "Thank you, God" or else we wholeheartedly express our discontent. We do that in a variety of ways. So, would you like to stop grumbling? Start thanking Him—for everything!

Besides, grumbling is forbidden by God in the Scriptures (Phil. 2:14). No circumstance is above this rule, so, there is no life situation that could justify grumbling. And by the way, God used to kill Israelites for it (Num. 11:1). Why is grumbling a sin? Because it is a sign of lack of trust in God. Grumbling is our rejection of his lordship, a kind of a spiritual rebellion. Grumbling is what are left with when we are not able to rebel physically. And secondly, grumbling is our rejection of God and His many attributes: wisdom, justice, love, faithfulness, omnipotence and omniscience. That's why grumbling is a serious offence against

God. In Job's case, his grumbling was directed against "injustice." But pain is not a good enough reason to shake your fists at the heavens. No agony gives us the right to resent God and murmur against Him. When we are tempted to cry out in indignation under the weight of incredible sufferings, let us remember that we are never without a choice. We will be greatly helped by realizing that grumbling will never alleviate our pain, but only aggravate it. By allowing ourselves to grumble, we embark on a journey through an endless desert, plodding along from one empty well to another. Isn't it better to learn the meekness of Christ and find the true peace for your soul (Matt. 11:29)? "Of course, it's better, but how do you humble yourself?" you may ask.

Humility

True humility is only possible when a person is ready to die to himself and to his earthly desires (Luke 14:33). Until then, he believes this earth to be the only source of happiness, and he will always have a lump in his throat as he thinks about his unfulfilled ambitions. He will be constantly tempted to grumble. The hardest thing for man is to humble himself without feeling any bitterness or resentment. People are proud by nature; pride lies at the core of all disobedience. So, if traced down to its root, every sin is caused by pride. Our Christian life starts when we humbly ask God for the forgiveness of our sins. Yes, humility is just as important for living this Christian life on a daily basis. There is more to the Gospel than just putting our faith in the sacrifice of Christ.

I would say the Gospel has two parts. The first part is the commandment to put your faith in the death and resurrection of Jesus Christ for the forgiveness of your sins (Acts 17:30). This is something that I personally embraced very quickly, and it was not very difficult. The difficult part of Christianity was the second part of the Gospel—the commandment to deny yourself. This became a real stumbling block; it just doesn't come easily. But the truth is, without this key element there's no Gospel. Jesus sets this condition quite clearly—to deny yourself, to die to yourself, in order to live for God. The whole New Testament is full of self-denial; in fact, it is there on every page! Thinking of Jesus as if he were just a supernatural psychotherapist whose only task is to bind up the wounded and meet people's needs is, of course, a stretch. Jesus is not simply added to our lives, his goal is to become our life. And to do it, he uses our circumstances, the very circumstances which invoke our greatest fears. We fast and pray, begging Him to rescue us from pain and trials, but He is using this very pain to break our rebellious hearts. Again and again, we hear the Gospel call from the pages of the Word of God—"Die to yourself!"

To humble yourself does not mean to no longer feel the pain of loss. To humble yourself means to reject despair, because despair is unbelief. It means to give up your right to a painless life, abandoning your own script for how things should be. To humble yourself means to give God the permission to do whatever He wishes with our lives, accepting any outcome of events. It is not sinful to cry out when you experience pain. But it is sinful to grumble. There is a clear difference between the two. The first one is okay, the second is not (Rom. 12:15; 1 Cor. 10:10).

The Worldly Hope

When all his hopes for the earthly bliss came to nothing, Job had yet another hope for something more substantial—eternal life. For a vast majority of people, the concept of eternal life is completely foreign. As we have already said above, it is our human nature to be dependent on something or someone, and each one chooses what to depend on. For a non-believer, who rejects God as the only source of hope, earth becomes the treasury of all good things. There is no third way; when we reject the Creator, all our hopes and dreams get refocused on creation. Let us, for the time being, call such hopes "worldly," meaning that they don't leave any room for God. The Scripture gives us the following list of the most sought-for objects of worldly hope:

- Money (Ps. 52:7);
- Government (Ps. 118:8–9);
- People (Is. 2:22; Jer. 17:5);
- Privileges (Phil. 3:4);
- Technology (Prov. 21:22);
- Idols, false gods (Is. 42:17);
- Military force (Is. 36:9).

The Bible continually speaks of vanity and unreliability of such hopes, and the history of the world bears its silent witness to this fact. If only people would learn from the mistakes of others yet they do not even learn from their own! Can anything from the above list save you from all the evils of the world? Of course not. None of these things rule the world, only God does! Yet people do not want God, and even those who turn to Him in times of trouble, usually look just for His help, not for God Himself. As soon as they get the help and relief, they turn their backs on Him (Ex. 9:27–35). The wicked irony is that even when people despise God as the only guarantor of eternal security, they still crave for security. In this unstable world, their biggest desire is for stability and security. Yet God made sure that people would never get peace here. The Earth is cursed (Gen. 3:17–19). Our everyday experience is ample evidence to the fact that there is no such thing as earthly security. Unforeseen life circumstances rule out any guarantees. Our plans can be thwarted at any moment. Even the most influential and powerful people walk under God, and are therefore limited in what they can do. Most of us understand this, and as a result there is fertile ground for superstitions.

Such a utilitarian way of viewing God expresses itself in various superstitions, among other things. It is amazing to see the degree of madness that a superstitious person can fall into when he tries to protect himself against the invisible supernatural forces—by adhering to the "safety rules." Generation after generation blindly repeats these "rules," without ever considering why in the world they do what they do. By the way, such "rules" exist in all the cultures of the world. I would define superstition as a fear of the supernatural without the fear of God. Typically, a superstitious person believes that there is an impersonal force of misfortune wandering the earth in search for its victims, and you can protect yourself against it by observing certain rituals. Simply put, all you need to do is to spit and tap at the right time and in the right place. And it doesn't really matter how you live. Such person believes that it is better to put on an amulet, knock on wood, and say a spell or two rather than turn to God and ask for protection. In his spiritual madness, he is ready to put his trust in whatever rather than go to God. Isn't it sheer insanity?

People tend to rely on anything, except God. That's why a man's whole life is nothing but a continuous disappointment in all his worldly objects of hope. It is a life of constant fear, because false hope cannot give real peace. Eventually, all our worldly hopes will fail and leave us helpless, miserable and broken, at the end of our rope. And beyond it lies the total darkness of eternal despair. This despair is well-deserved, because those who have rejected the redeeming grace of God must eventually experience life without a single manifestation of God's goodness, including hope. The word "hope" is not in the vocabulary of those who dwell in hell.

While we live on Earth, we continue to hope, each in his own way. We always expect something good to happen, and we say, "I hope that [fill in the blank]." Usually this is an expression of some anticipation, which may or may not be fulfilled. Some hopes are supported by specific promises, but it still doesn't mean that they will come true. So the word "hope," in most cases, is used to express uncertainty. For situations where the outcome is unquestionable, other words are used, such as: confidence, guarantees, inevitability, etc.

The Biblical Hope

In the Bible, hope has nothing to do with uncertainty and is in no way connected to worldly expectations. Biblical hope is the *assurance* of eternal life based on God's promise. This promise refers to the time of the return of Jesus Christ in glory for the establishment of His Kingdom, and includes a personal resurrection and coming into the inheritance in heaven. In other words, it is our guarantee of eternal life. And it is based on a simple fact that there is God's promise behind it (Tit. 1:2–3, Heb. 6:13–20). Besides, this hope is personal. Our hope is Jesus Christ Himself (1 Tim. 1:1; Col. 1:26–27). It's not a horseshoe hung over the door, nor an amulet or a sacred tree. You can talk to Him.

In this vein, the Bible points out that unbelievers have no hope whatsoever (1 Thess. 4:13, Eph. 2:12). The implication is that all their hopes will end with death, because eternal life, obviously, is not something a worldly person looks forward to. For them it makes perfect sense—the idea of resurrection from the dead is sheer insanity for the lost world. But for us, the resurrection of Jesus Christ is the hope of our own resurrection (1 Pet. 1:3–5). Note this: long before the doctrine of the resurrection of the body was formulated in the Scripture, Job had already put it in the foundation of his hope: "As for me, I know that my Redeemer lives, and at the last He will take His stand on the earth. Even after my skin is destroyed, yet from my flesh I shall see God" (19:25–26). Isn't is surprising that this pre-Old Testament patriarch points out the two key elements of the authentic biblical hope: redemption and the resurrection of the dead. See how confident Job is— "I *know* . . ." Because of this knowledge he was able to keep all despair at bay.

There is a world of difference between the earthly and heavenly hope. In times of trial, the former proves frail and unreliable, while the latter proves unshakable. Soviet authors Alexander Solzhenitsyn and Varlam Shalamov both describe their lives as inmates in Stalin's gulags. They both refer to this curious fact that Christians were often among those who were able to retain their humanity even in the face of most inhuman sufferings. In a letter to Solzhenitsyn, Shalamov, an atheist, gives the following surprising characteristic of believers:[3]

> "In the course of the twenty years spent in labor camps, I formed one strong opinion which is the sum total of my lifelong observations: the people who were able to retain their authentic human traits in the face of all the atrocities, starvation, beatings, freezing temperatures, and hard labor were sectarians and the 'religious folk' in general, including Orthodox priests. Of course, there were some good people from other 'layers of society,' but it was more of an exception—and they would often break when their hardships escalated. Yes, sectarians always remained truly human."[4]

---

[3] Shalamov calls Christians "sectarians" and "the religious folk."

[4] V. T. Shalamov, in a letter to Solzhenitsyn. November, 1962. Quoted from: http://www.booksite.ru/fulltext/new/boo/ksh/ala/mov/60.htm (accessed: 11.Aug.2010).

Chapter 5. Hope

What is the secret of their stamina? The answer is simple: their faith in God and hope for a better future. It is not a groundless or blind hope which tells a person that he has to somehow survive the present hell, and then, finally, "he will live as a normal person," but a profound biblical assurance, which keeps the despair from entering the soul, no matter how much it tries to break in. The biblical hope will keep us afloat even when everyone around is drowning in total darkness.

A worldview which excludes God and rejects the hope of a better future after death is purely situational, feeble and uncertain, without a foundation and a true meaning. The value of such a worldview is inextricably connected to this earthly life. The person will seek his joy exclusively in the earthly realm, in the horizontal dimension, and any sufferings will be seen by him as obstacles to happiness. They are an enemy. What's the point in enduring hardship when you know that you have nothing but this day to justify your existence? There's no point in being godly and abstain from fleshly desires, if this life is all you have. The nature of all worldly hopes can be put in two words: HERE and NOW! There is only here and now, so morality is also purely situational and contextual. People give all of their energy to satisfying their immediate desires. Despite all disappointments, they still, like newborn kittens, blindly crawl around in search for the one thing that will bring them the ultimate satisfaction. After they find something, they rejoice and revel in their happiness for some time, but then see that their "precious" has lost its glamor. Oh no! Even the most cherished toy will ultimately cease to satisfy. The search is resumed. They set new attractive goals and aspirations, hoping to quench the thirst for the meaning of life, but even if this new goal is reached, the cycle will repeat it. This way of life is an incessant rat race! Solomon called it "chasing after the wind." Vanity!

What an awful state of mind it must be to suddenly realize that the "here and now" is forever gone, or for some reason is inaccessible. What then can protect you from despair? Nothing but hope in God. Yet people run away from God. They deal with the frightening and intrusive thoughts (as well as with the sense of guilt) in the same way they deal with any other pain—by taking painkillers. The list of painkillers is constantly growing, but some of the most popular are alcohol, drugs, sex, food, work, art and entertainment. These surrogate joys help to sooth the pain and "fill up" the intolerable spiritual void in the heart. Deprived of any hope, the person will cling to these things just like a baby clings to a pacifier, yet he will inevitably go to his end. Some do not even wait for death, but take their own lives to escape the devastating and painful sensation of total meaninglessness.

Promises

False beliefs come in the absence of truth. Jesus said to the Sadducees in response to their silly question, "You are mistaken, not understanding the Scriptures nor the power of God" (Matt. 22:29). The result of misinterpreting the Word of God is a false theology, particularly, a distorted perception of some of God's promises. False promises will give rise to false expectations, and false expectations will lead to disappointments we just mentioned. When truth is neglected, people's expectations of God and of life are generally ungrounded. It's tragic to see so many Christians finding promises in the Bible that the Lord never gave. We are especially quick in spotting promises about a secure life in this world (health, wealth, and success). Believers must be absolutely convinced about what God actually promised. When the Scripture is not studied but just read in a superficial way, it is impossible to avoid certain hermeneutical pitfalls which will result in theological errors and then in actions which a person will regret.

Chapter 5. Hope

I know people who attended church for a long time, prayed fervently, knew the Scriptures well enough, preached the gospel with courage, but finally turned away from God because of some resentment or anger. He disappointed them by not giving them what they had asked for. In my opinion, such people are more miserable than atheists, because non-believers may still come to God when life gets hard, but the former have already "tasted" the Lord and found Him distasteful. Such is a fate of all who come to God for something else besides the forgiveness of sins. But those who call upon the Lord under the crushing burden of their sins, who hate the filth of their own souls, who are tired of their moral deformity, will NEVER leave Jesus Christ, because this is exactly what God promised to help them with! Will those who yearn for holiness ever be disappointed in the Lord? Never!

So, let us look at the actual promises found in the Bible. The first and the foremost is the promise mentioned above—the promise of the forgiveness of sins and eternal life with God (Acts 10:43, Tit. 1:2). This is the greatest gift of all—all the other promises pale in comparison with this one. But unfortunately, Christians rarely reflect on this wonderful biblical promise on a regular basis. If we really appreciated the gift of eternal life, all the other promises would have faded into insignificance. Whoever has learned to be happy in the knowledge that God in Christ has forgiven all our sins, that the Destroyer has passed over, and that the gates of heaven have been flung opened, will not bother God with petty requests for earthly blessings! For such a person all his temporary adversities will seem manageable. The following illustration comes to mind:

Imagine that you are the captain of a coast guard boat. One day after a storm, you spot a half-dead young man overboard, in the middle of the Pacific Ocean. The crew pulls him onboard and performs first aid. The poor fellow is in terrible condition. Completely exhausted, he sincerely thanks you for saving him.

You want to take good care of him, so you provide him with a separate cabin to rest in, and bring a doctor to examine him. After a while, you visit your newly acquired friend and find him healthy and full of energy. Wonderful! But as you start chatting, he immediately mentions that he would like a bigger and nicer cabin. You are surprised, but you tell him you will do your best to help. As you proceed, you see that your guest is constantly demanding more and more. Now he wants a phone and an Internet connection. Now he is complaining about not getting the nutritious food he needs, and asks for his own TV. In tears, he tells you how unfairly he is treated on the ship—that he is not even allowed to come up to the steering wheel, or push the buttons, or pull the levers. He is unhappy about the choppy waters, the cold and damp weather, and the monotonous view out his window. On top of it all, he resentfully declares that if you had been a really good captain, you would have given up your cabin for him.

What would you have done if you were the captain of the ship? I'd probably be feeling a strong temptation to throw this brazen jerk overboard. You might say, "If I were in his place, I would never have been so outrageously ungrateful!" But let me tell you this; you are mostly likely already outrageously ungrateful, and quite often. If you are offended at God for something, if you grumble or accuse him of not taking care of you, if you get frustrated when you endure hardship, or simply mope over not getting your expectations met, then you, probably, are that young man in our story. Why would we often act this way instead of constantly keeping in mind that we were in the middle of that raging, bottomless, and cold abyss from which we were miraculously saved, and gratefully accepting whatever conditions we are offered on board the ship that is taking us Home? Isn't it a monstrous ingratitude? Let us not grieve the heavenly Captain with our incessant grumbling, but rather let us make ourselves useful on this wonderful ship because there's so much to do. Let us often look at the Cross, anticipating our glorious future in Heaven and saying together with the apostle Paul:

> "Therefore we do not lose heart, but though our outer man is decaying, yet our inner man is being renewed day by day. For momentary, light affliction is producing for us an eternal weight of glory far beyond all comparison, while we look not at the things which are seen, but at the things which are not seen; for the things which are seen are temporal, but the things which are not seen are eternal." (2 Cor. 4:16–18)

Let us say together with the apostle Peter:

> "Blessed be the God and Father of our Lord Jesus Christ, who according to His great mercy has caused us to be born again to a living hope through the resurrection of Jesus Christ from the dead, to obtain an inheritance which is imperishable and undefiled and will not fade away, reserved in heaven for you, who are protected by the power of God through faith for a salvation ready to be revealed in the last time. In this you greatly rejoice, even though now for a little while, if necessary, you have been distressed by various trials." (1 Pet. 1:3–6)

Let me also list other important biblical promises:

1. Answer to prayer/petition (1 John 5:14–15). But does God promise to give us WHATEVER we ask for? No. There's a good qualifier here: we should only be asking according to His will.

2. Victory over sin (1 Cor. 10:13). Do we always prevail over sin? No. Who is to blame when we fall into sin? We are. Because God does not lie, and He promised that He would not allow us to be tempted beyond our ability to endure.

3. Guidance (Prov. 3:5–6). Who is guilty when we do something that ultimately gets us in trouble? Just look in the mirror.

4. Promise to never leave us or forsake us, no matter what (Heb. 13:5). What if you feel like God has left you? You will have to choose who to believe, yourself or God. But don't forget who, according to the Scriptures, will be found a liar (Rom. 3:4).

Does God promise to protect me from every evil person in the world? No! On the contrary, He assures me that "... all who desire to live godly in Christ Jesus will be persecuted" (2 Tim. 3:12). And how do you feel about such a promise? The Apostle Paul endured multiple beatings, humiliations, and contempt. Does God promise us wealth or that we will always have enough? No. On the contrary, he is preparing us for all sorts of things, saying: "If we have food and covering, with these we shall be content" (1 Tim. 6:8). There were times of dire need in the life of the Apostle Paul (Phil. 4:12). Does God promise us good health and protection from every illness? Not at all! Paul's faithful assistant and a co-worker Epaphroditus nearly died of illness, and even Paul himself was not able to heal him. Timothy, Paul's beloved co-laborer, suffered from stomach problems and was often sick (1 Tim. 5:23). There are also discussions among theologians as to the nature of Paul's own ailment (2 Cor. 12:7–8; Gal. 4:15; Gal. 6:11).

So, let us look the reality in the face without ransacking the Word of God for guarantees of a comfortable, healthy and secure life on earth. You won't find any! There is only one thing guaranteed—the hope of the glory of God (Rom. 5:1–2). Stop looking for lasting happiness in this life. Stop chasing after the wind. When you are overfocused on your earthly existence, grumbling is unavoidable, because God, who resists the proud, will make sure that you have your share of disappointments. Reject the "here and now." Replace it with: "THERE and THEN," for

"... where your treasure is your heart will be also" (Matt. 6:21). For such a radical shift of focus, FAITH is the absolute necessity! Do you have it? Job had it and remained faithful to God in spite of his losses! He was sustained by hope—that same biblical hope for eternal joy, which surpasses all the temporary hardships and trials on this earth.

> *For in hope we have been saved,*
> *but hope that is seen is not hope;*
> *for who hopes for what he already sees?*
> *But if we hope for what we do not see,*
> *with perseverance we wait eagerly for it.*
> *(Rom. 8:24–25)*

6

THE "RIGHTEOUS" REBELLION

In the previous chapter we saw how strong was Job's temptation to start grumbling. We also discussed the importance of having biblical hope. It is quite clear that this righteous man gave himself the permission to have "a little" rebellion. We find Job a patient man but also an angry man. As he pours out his soul, he often contradicts himself, speaks emotionally, cries out in desperation and weeps many tears. Don't forget that this man was utterly exhausted, both physically and emotionally. He was totally emaciated, looking like a bag of bones (19:20). His body was covered with festering wounds (7:5). He couldn't sleep, and when he fell asleep, he had nightmares (7:4, 13–14). He was constantly weeping (16:16). This was a miserable life, a waking hell, without a hint of relief (9:18). And on top of it, he was totally alone, even though he had his friends with him. Few people have gone through a similarly excruciating experience. One thing is clear,

Job was not crushed, he did not lose his faith or abandon his righteousness. "Nevertheless the righteous will hold to his way, and he who has clean hands will grow stronger and stronger" (17:9).

Satan did everything in his power to draw the curse out of Job's lips. And curse he did! Only he didn't curse God, oh no! Job cursed the day of his birth (3:1–13), but he wasn't able to go beyond that—he had the fear of God.[1] So, should we see these words just as the overflow of emotions, without any hidden agenda behind them? Hardly. He expressed a desire not to have been born, which is quite understandable in light of the fact that he was struggling to make any sense of God's actions. "Why is light given to a man whose way is hidden, and whom God has hedged in?" (3:23). He was terrified by God's behavior—not so much by the tragedy itself but by the absence of any rational explanation for it.

> "For He performs what is appointed for me, and many such decrees are with Him. Therefore, I would be dismayed at His presence; when I consider, I am terrified of Him. It is God who has made my heart faint, and the Almighty who has dismayed me, But I am not silenced by the darkness, nor deep gloom which covers me." (23:14–17)

In cursing the day of his birth, Job also cursed God's plan for his life. Indirectly he put the blame on God for the meaninglessness of his existence, as if saying that the Lord made a mistake in creating him and allotting him such a long life. His words seem to imply, "Why should I live now that I am destined to die such a cruel death?" His mind ran into an insurmountable conundrum

---

[1] George M. Schwab, "The Book of Job and Counsel in the Whirlwind," *Journal of Biblical Counseling* 17, 1 (Fall 1998):34.

of God's mystery, and his constant physical and emotional anguish prevented him from thinking straight. It was so hard to comprehend what was going on, much less to recover the lost meaning of life and restore his relationship with the Creator.

In the state of extreme physical and spiritual exhaustion, it was incredibly difficult to not jump to conclusions about God in total despair (Satan knows how to break a man). Job sincerely tried to make any sense out of God's actions, but was at a total loss. And this was the most painful thing of all, that he was trying to understand God but couldn't! It is meaninglessness that makes our suffering unbearable. We throw in the towel and lose all motivation to go on. "I am guiltless; I do not take notice of myself. I despise my life. It is all one; therefore I say, 'He destroys the guiltless and the wicked'" (9:21–22).

Do you see the utter desperation behind these words? Job felt as if the fine line between good and evil was being erased before his very eyes. He no longer saw any difference between the righteous and the wicked—since God himself didn't seem to differentiate between the two. The orderly world Job knew collapsed before his very eyes, and all its laws were in a total mess. Where is right and where is left? Where is the bottom and where is the top? What is good and what is bad? On the verge of insanity, Job exclaims in confusion, "God, what's going on? Are you the God I have always known? You seem to have changed! I no longer understand you! I am at a loss! I am afraid of you! Why live if you are like this? End my life now" (cf. 6:9).

It must be admitted that, unlike the Israelites on the way out of Egypt, Job had every reason to grumble—from the purely human point of view. Compared to Job's circumstances, all the hardships of the Israelites during their exodus are but a hiking tour led by the professional guide Moses. In spite of the constant flow of revelations and God's personal presence and protection, in spite of God's total predictability and unfailing daily provisions, they had the nerve to grumble. What incredible arrogance! Job was absolutely alone. He was in what I would call a "theological and informational isolation" and suffered immensely. Besides, he was terrified of God who had suddenly ceased to be "adequate." It seemed to him that God had suddenly gone insane. So, Job's grumbling is not the result of cowardly unbelief (as it was in the case of Jews in the desert), but rather a consequence of his theological impasse. In some mysterious supernatural way, he continued to worship the One whom he had ceased to understand. Only by faith was he able to get out of his mire. Job was a truly great man!

Even in this miserable state, he was honest with himself and saw right through the rebellious nature of his own complaints.

> "I loathe my own life; I will give full vent to my complaint;
> I will speak in the bitterness of my soul." (10:1)

> "Even today my complaint is rebellion;[2]
> His hand is heavy despite my groaning." (23:2)

Job gave himself the permission to have a bloodless coup, which he would later regret because in so doing he would go too far. At first, he kept his mouth shut so as to avoid sinning, but then he caved in and opened himself up to despair. I will say it again—his despair was fully understandable from a human point of view, the man was in agony. But what does "understandable" mean here? Does it mean it could be justified? How should we, in general, view Job's reaction to his trials? Technically, nothing blasphemous came out of his lips. So why does he eventually repent of his own words? Why does he "retract and repent in dust and ashes" (42:6)?

---

[2] The primary meaning of this word is "defiant."

Sinning Through Tears

Towards the end of the book, God starts a conversation with Job. From the very first words we see that, in spite of the horrible sufferings endured by Job, God does not condone his rebellious speeches. True, Job wished to sue God, but he was in a lot of pain. His reasoning must have been clouded by this incredible stress, so why take his words so seriously? Couldn't God just sweep it under the rug, considering that Job remained faithful and did not renounce his Creator? No, He couldn't.

The most loving being in the universe reveals Himself in a terrible storm and instills fear in the heart of His most faithful servant exactly at the time when Job needed comfort the most (38:1). When I was anticipating God's response to Job's entreaties, I was imagining how He would gently embrace the poor soul and comfort him with many, many words of consolation. I was ready see God sitting down next to Job in the dirt and weeping with him. What I read didn't square at all with my idea of good counsel. "Good grief!" I thought to myself. "Is this heavenly mercy?" "How about 'weep with those who weep?'" I mused. "Lord, where's your compassion?" I was beside myself.

It was a while before I realized that this was exactly what true compassion does. The wise God offered Job what he needed most at the moment. This was a sobering slap in the face, because he had gone too far in his complaints by forgetting that even pain does not entitle one to sin. Accusing God of injustice and wishing to sue Him was a sin!

Compassion is a good thing. It is what the Lord commanded us to do (Rom. 12:15). But you cannot have your will and reasoning be morally paralyzed by someone's pain. We must learn how to empathize in accordance with the truth, in any given situation, because when we are not led by the Spirit, we are led by the flesh (Gal. 5:16). There's no third option. When compassion originates in our flesh, we are only concerned with reducing the suffering and providing relief. And if it's necessary to blame and accuse God to do so, so be it. There are many Christians who are well-read in modern psychotherapy who would claim that getting rid of negative emotions is very important.[3] Even if one had to chuck the Lord of Lords Himself for the sake of emotional venting, it's not much of a problem.[4] After all, it will bring the person the desired peace of mind, and this is what our fleshly compassion is primarily concerned with.

"Christian" Psychology

As we continue our study of the Book of Job, I would like to add a few words on the topic of Christian psychology. Here's why; Christian psychologists would claim that the kind of help that God offered Job was absolutely inappropriate (maybe that's why I have never read any Christian psychologist's comments on the last chapters of the book of Job). God's "approach" to Job seems to smash to smithereens the most foundational principles of this type of counseling.[5] Before I start, let me describe this semi-Christian field in general terms. There is one conversation in the Bible, which, in my opinion, perfectly illustrates the point

---

[3] L. P. Bradford, J. R. Gibb, and K. D. Benne, *T-group Theory and Laboratory Method* (New York: John Wiley and Sons, Inc., 1964), p. 206.

[4] Marilyn Murray, *Prisoner of Another War: A Remarkable Journey of Healing From Childhood Trauma* (Berkley: PageMill Press, 1991), pp. 85, 114.

[5] Christian psychology is not the same as biblical counseling. They are two entirely different things. The major difference between them is that they rely on different sources of authority. Biblical counseling relies solely on the Word of God in serving the needs of the suffering souls (the 66 canonical books). Christian psychology uses not only the Word of God but also their own psychological findings and techniques, thus ascribing the two the same level of authority.

I am trying to make. Let us, for a brief moment, put down the Book of Job and turn to the dialogue between Peter and Jesus after the Lord had told His disciples about how His earthly life was going to end,

> "From that time Jesus began to show His disciples that He must go to Jerusalem, and suffer many things from the elders and chief priests and scribes, and be killed, and be raised up on the third day. Peter took Him aside and began to rebuke Him, saying, 'God forbid it, Lord! This shall never happen to You.'" (Matt. 16:21–22)

As we see, Peter, out of the best of intentions, was trying to prevent his Teacher from hurting Himself, literally rebuking Him for the desire to die. To Peter's surprise, Jesus responded to his "caring admonition" in the following way:

> "But He turned and said to Peter, 'Get behind Me, Satan! You are a stumbling block to Me; for you are not setting your mind on God's interests, but man's.'" (Matt. 16:23)

Peter gets a sharp reprimand instead of words of gratitude and teary eyes. And also, he gets a strange name. It must have been a while before he was able to get over the shock. Did Peter understand what was going on? Did he understand why he got the rebuke? Ultimately, he did. And we will understand it as well.

Note well what Jesus is saying here, in verse twenty-one. There are at least three parts to His message: (1) He "must suffer many things from the elders and chief priests . . ." (2) He "must be killed . . ." (3) He "must be raised up on the third day." What did Peter "get" from this message? Just the first two parts—that Christ had to suffer many things and be killed. Why is that? The message was wrapped up with the most beautiful words: ". . . must be raised on the third day"! It seems like every time Jesus spoke about his resurrection, the disciples became hard of hearing. Why wasn't he ever asked, "Jesus, you have just mentioned something about your being raised on the third day. Did I hear that correctly? Wow! Wonderful! Could you, please, share more about this interesting concept?"

We see nothing of the kind. The disciples seemed unable to hear some of the most important things in the teaching of Jesus. But it is a whole other topic. Let us note for now that in this case Jesus himself explains the reason for this "inability to hear," "... for you are not setting your mind on God's interests, but man's." This episode is a fine example of how our fleshly compassion operates—it sets its mind on the interests of man, not God. But it is only natural—our flesh is unable to look forward to the kingdom come. Fleshly mind is set on earthly things. Such an "earthly" approach to life will always lead a person to sell his birthright for a bowl of lentils, for this miserably short earthly existence. It's not possible to please the Lord if your heart is set on pleasing men.

The core of Christian psychology can be summed up by the following phrase: "... for you are not setting your mind on God's interests, but man's." The followers of this worldly teaching are so preoccupied with comforting men that they totally forget about the One they should be pleasing above all else. When they offer their "therapy," they see pain as the main culprit, and in so doing ignore the gravity of human sin. When Peter was giving Jesus his piece of advice, he wasn't really thinking about the will of God, and that God might be pleased with sending His Son to die.

Peter just wanted to show compassion—yet Jesus rejected his help. By offering this solution, the close disciple of Jesus basically claimed that he was more compassionate than God the Father. Let us ask ourselves this question; can anyone be more merciful than God? Obviously not—it's a rhetorical question. Our human compassion, when it neglects God's commandment, always ends up in perpetrating cruelty. For instance, parents who are overprotective with their children, will never discipline them properly, and will never love them the way they should. It would not be love but hate—based on the biblical perspective (Prov. 13:25). Peter wanted to help in the same way Christian psychologists help their clients. But what would have happened if Jesus had listened to Peter's advice and spared Himself? He would have disobeyed His Father, not to mention the dire consequences that such an act would have entailed. Where would we be now?

In God's eyes, the main culprit is our sin, not our pain. God's compassion means that He will empathize with us in our pain, but will only offer the kind of help which does not contradict the Father's will. Biblical compassion weeps with those who weep, but won't indulge our sins, regardless of how many tears we have shed. Biblical compassion rebukes with gentleness and carries the other person's burdens, but will never condone sin (Gal. 6:1-2). When a Christian learns to fear sin more than pain, we can be sure that Christ has been formed in him. When dealing with their own or someone else's pain, the children of God should emulate Christ's example. True compassion is a thing to be learned.

God appeared to Job in the storm to bring him true compassion. We see that He didn't exactly praise Job for his honesty, nor did He approve of Job's sincerity in pouring out his negative emotions like a "healthy individual" would. This is the first major difference between God's counseling and Christian psychology. In Christian psychology, emotional suppression is believed to produce psychological trauma—this is something they share with their secular colleagues. So, some of them would teach the kind of "sincerity" before God which gives you a license to freely vent your emotional state, even if your heart is full of hatred and curses towards God.

The Trust Dilemma

If suppressing your emotions (like anger) is unwise and harmful, then we have a trust dilemma. We can either trust the "psychology experts," or the Word of God—they invariably contradict each other. Scripture says, "A fool always loses his temper, but a wise man holds it back" (Prov. 29:11). The psychologists' claim that suppression of anger has an adverse effect on both mental and physical health proceeds from an erroneous anthropology, which is based on Freud (in this particular case) rather than on Scripture. If they knew the truth about human nature, they would never have prescribed such a course of actions.

One of the problems of this approach is that "sincere" pouring out of anger may help a person to have a temporary "cleansing" (a kind of mental catharsis), but he or she will eventually develop a sinful habit of flying into rage. My observations have brought me to the conclusion that psychological treatment brings greater harm to patients compared to their initial states. The idea is to help a person to get rid of anger through venting, but in the end, I found that the person just becomes angrier and more irritable. By refusing to keep himself in check, he indulges his sinful flesh and obeys its evil desires—whatever the psychologists might say. It's like watering weeds in a warm season. The thorns will only grow faster when they receive the water they need—sending their roots deeper and continuing to multiply. Or they might say that by venting difficult emotions through tears the person will, in the end, feel more joy. In reality, however, he or she will become even more miserable and will cry over every trifle so as to not "suppress" anything and cause more trauma.

So, the effect of such a "treatment" is exactly opposite to what might have been expected. The person gradually becomes less emotionally stable and more erratic, less sacrificial and more selfish, less spiritual and more carnal. He or she is focused on getting their "essential" needs met, like self-fulfillment, feeling of significance, love and security. They develop an appetite for the "daily bread" of psychology. It is so sad to watch the growing popularity of the so-called Christian therapy for groups and individuals where self-obsessed people get together to bemoan their wounded pride. In such therapy sessions, they do not accept their pain as something that came from God, but rather try to adapt to it by means of psychological and theological manipulations. They prepare themselves to face life's misfortunes by means of psychological tools which help them to maintain mental balance—by setting healthy boundaries, learning to express your emotions, articulating your inner states, and figuring out your own and someone else's motives.

Choice

Our earthly suffering is real—I don't wish to downplay this. However, some people might conclude that pain and trials are an excuse to act "unspiritually," and that a suffering person doesn't have a choice but to rebel (just like Job). The truth is that, although we cannot prevent certain things from happening, we can still control our reactions. That's why we are fully responsible before God for our behavior. Nothing and no one can force a Christian to act in a certain way until he or she chooses to do so. We may be under physical and spiritual pressure, but the ability to make choices remains. In the end, the decision will be made based on our moral principles. When we are in a crucible, we can't help but show our true theological convictions.

Let us consider the following example of how Jesus made the right choice even under much pressure. When he was tempted in the wilderness, he put the Father's will above all his legitimate human needs and desires (Matt. 4:1–4). He fasted for forty days.

How many of us know what that feels like? Very few. He had a very specific physical need—hunger. And this is what Satan put his stakes on, in order to influence his decision. However, this did not in any way turn Jesus away from the agony of slowly dying—He chose to remain faithful to the Father. Jesus felt that in this case, even starvation was not a good enough reason to sin. He chose to go hungry but remain obedient to His Father.

Who among us is ready, following the footsteps of the Savior, to go without food for the sake of pleasing God? Who among us fears disobeying God more than the pains of physical exhaustion, relational hunger, sexual abstinence, or any other form of deprivation? Who among us is determined to endure to the end, even when a dire temptation threatens to choke us in its vile grip? Initially, we all resist for some time, but when the increasing pressures of the flesh become unbearable, we turn to flight. Sooner or later we surrender, not wishing to experience this terrible sensation of an unfulfilled desire. It seems quite absurd in light of the fact that these unpleasant but temporary troubles don't kill anybody (unless we are talking about physical starvation), but we still deem them more terrifying than giving an account to the Lord for all our actions. Seems highly unreasonable.

Once I was approached by a "believer" who shared with me that he had left his wife after she had refused to give him physical intimacy. He was sincerely trying to convince me that he had no other choice. He was looking to me to give him the sympathy he wanted and justification for his actions, but, of course, he did not get any. As a fellow man, I can understand his troubles, but as a Christian I cannot, and do not wish to justify his choice. Why? Is it because I'm cruel? Not at all! Is it because I'm perfect? Not in the least! I wouldn't condone his sin simply because . . . God does not condone it! What difference does it make whether I pardon his actions or not? Does it really matter? After all, I'm only human! He will have to give an account to God, not to me.

Chapter 6. The "Righteous" Rebellion

In such a case, rebuking the person is the best possible way to show compassion, because by exposing his sin we remind him of the imminent danger of God's judgement. We are helping him to shift his focus from the temporary to the eternal. This is exactly what Jesus did to Peter by reminding him of the One whom we should please above all. I'm learning compassion from God himself—regardless of what my feelings are. The heart can indeed bleed to death at the sight of someone's pain, but it is at this moment that we need to show compassion according to God's will. Feelings are fleeting and deceitful, but God's Word is eternal and true.

In other words, the Lord does not need our explanations for why we committed a sin; The Creator demonstrated zero tolerance toward sin as early as the Garden of Eden, when He refused to accept excuses from Adam and Eve. That's why we also should stop justifying ourselves. It is quite pointless. What's the use of trying to convince people that you had no other choice? Will you be able to change God's mind? And what about Job? Did he have the right to rebel in such desperate circumstances? The answer is no. This ancient book also teaches us that no actions on the part of God give us the license to question his justice, kindness and wisdom. Whatever happens, God wants us to have humble, submissive, and grateful hearts. Naturally, for someone like Job, who was in terrible agony, it might sound like a mockery. Our desire to praise God does not come automatically in times of trial, and if you just passively wait for it to appear, you might have to wait a very long time. All you need to do is start doing it, that is, start praising. And it doesn't mean you need to experience any particular elation or excitement at the moment of doing it. After all, we all get up in the morning and go to work, even if our emotional state leaves much to be desired. We just get dressed and go. Not going to work is not an option! People are universally motivated by the desire for earthly security and wellbeing. In other words, when we are properly motivated, we can do things that we do not like.

From the Bible's point of view, the right motivation is our desire to please the Lord. When we are faced with a difficult question of whether to keep worshiping the Lord in times of trouble, we always have a choice—to do what we feel like, or to do what is right. To follow our emotions or to do the Lord's bidding. Even non-believers can see this essential difference, and they choose to do the former, as a rule. For example, when the head of a family leaves his wife and children for another woman, he *knows* that, objectively speaking, he is doing something wrong, but that does not stop him. At this moment, he is acting based on the principle "I want this—I don't want that," not the principle "this is good and that is bad." His desire for a woman who isn't his wife is his ultimate authority. For him, his own happiness is more important than the miserable situation he is subjecting his children and wife to. For him, it is less acceptable to deny himself some sinful pleasure than abandon his family to the mercy of fate. He is a spiritually dead man, and his actions proceed from his hardness of heart. Why then do we as Christians choose to act according to our feelings and not according to the truth? Why aren't we motivated by the desire to please the Lord just like we are motivated by the desire to secure our earthly prosperity? The answer is simple; our old nature demands that we please ourselves, not God. The life credo with which we were born into the world runs like this—my will be done! Such a system of priorities is the best proof that our self-esteem is fine and that we have an all-conquering love for ourselves.

The next premise of Christian psychology, which falls apart in light of the book of Job, is this: each person has an intrinsic objective value (in the eyes of God), but we often underestimate ourselves because of low self-esteem. In other words, God values people very highly, but because we cannot fully grasp it, it causes us all sorts of troubles. We will discuss the topic of our objective value in the next two chapters. For now, let us go back to self-esteem which is so popular nowadays.

Self-esteem

The world-famous Christian psychologist James Dobson builds his counseling system on the premise that everyone has low self-esteem. Dobson asserts, "Self-esteem is the most vulnerable of all human attributes; it is so easily damaged and it is so hard to restore."[6] He also states that, "Indeed, low self-esteem is a global threat."[7] Does the Bible have anything to say about low self-esteem? Yes, of course! It denies this concept altogether. In the pages of the Holy Scripture, God's people evaluate themselves in such a way that any psychologist would diagnose them with "unhealthy self-esteem." The statements of prophets and apostles seem to indicate that they all had serious problems with self-esteem.

> "I am unworthy of all the lovingkindness and of all the faithfulness which You have shown to Your servant; for with my staff only I crossed this Jordan, and now I have become two companies." (Gen. 32:10)

> "Behold, I was brought forth in iniquity, and in sin my mother conceived me." (Ps. 51:5)

> "And he was preaching, and saying, 'After me One is coming who is mightier than I, and I am not fit to stoop down and untie the thong of His sandals.'" (Mark 1:7).

---

[6]James Dobson, *Dare to Discipline* (Wheaton, IL: Tyndale House Pub., 1970), p. 19.

[7]James Dobson, *What Wives Wish Their Husbands Knew about Women* (Wheaton, IL: Tyndale House Pub., 1975), p. 28.

> "It is a trustworthy statement, deserving full acceptance, that Christ Jesus came into the world to save sinners, among whom I am foremost of all." (1 Tim. 1:15)

Please note that in all of the Bible God never tries to persuade us otherwise. In fact, He confirms the words of these men and women of God:

> "So you too, when you do all the things which are commanded you, say, 'We are unworthy slaves; we have done only that which we ought to have done.'" (Luke 17:10)

We don't find a single statement, rebuke or command in the Bible addressed to people with low self-esteem. All the rebukes are for those who have a very high self-esteem.

> "For through the grace given to me I say to everyone among you not to think more highly of himself than he ought to think; but to think so as to have sound judgment, as God has allotted to each a measure of faith." (Rom. 12:3)

> "Do not judge so that you will not be judged. For in the way you judge, you will be judged; and by your standard of measure, it will be measured to you. Why do you look at the speck that is in your brother's eye, but do not notice the log that is in your own eye?" (Matt. 7:1–3)

> "Do nothing from selfishness or empty conceit, but with humility of mind regard one another as more important than yourselves. Do not merely look out for your own personal interests, but also for the interests of others." (Phil. 2:3–4)

> "In everything, therefore, treat people the same way you want them to treat you, for this is the Law and the Prophets." (Matt. 7:12)

For people with low self-esteem, the first three admonitions would sound something like this: "Do not think about yourself worse than you are, but think of yourself highly, in accordance with your true value." "Why do you look at the speck in your own eye, and do not notice the log in your brother's eye?" "Do nothing out of low self-esteem, but, esteeming yourself as you should, regard yourself no worse than others. Do not merely look out for the interests of others, but also for your own interests." Have you ever read in the Scriptures anything like this? I haven't! On the contrary, it is clearly stated: "For no one ever hated his own flesh, but nourishes and cherishes it . . ." (Eph. 5:29). It is quite curious that the list of the sins of those who will live in last days starts with lovers of self (2 Tim. 3:1–5). And what about Job's self-esteem? Let's see how this paragon of virtue saw himself so we can imitate his example? It turns out that he also suffered from a "low self-esteem:"

"Behold, I am insignificant; what can I reply to You?
I lay my hand on my mouth." (40:4)

From the point of view of Christian psychology, God should have said after such words, "Oh no, no, Job! Don't say that! It hurts my ears when you belittle yourself like this. I forbid you to think badly of yourself!" No, God did not even try to talk His faithful servant out of it. On the contrary, he reminded him again and again of his low status. Everything in the Word of God and in our lives testifies to the fact that we tend to value and love ourselves more than others. Is the Lord's command to deny yourself given to people with low self-esteem? Nothing of the kind! Would it be so difficult for someone who really thinks little of himself to give up everything and follow God? Not at all! Is it so difficult for a person with low self-esteem to forgive others or ask for forgiveness? By no means. Can there be a real conflict between spouses who truly suffer from low self-esteem? Well, maybe—if they want to argue over the right to do all the hard work. Any conflict between two or more people is the result of clashing wills. If you really have low self-esteem, you will always deny your insignificant desires and choose someone else's will to obey. However, conflict arises when we insist, "My will be done," because we consider ourselves to be more important than the other party. Or let us examine the purely human phenomenon of *self-justification,* which originated back in the Garden of Eden. Wouldn't you say that self-justification often accompanies our "repentance" when we have a high view of ourselves? Isn't it logically inconsistent for a person with a low self-esteem to turn to self-justification? Only those who think highly of themselves feel entitled to defend themselves! *Making excuses means that you are trying to save face when your moral character is under scrutiny.* So making excuses basically means, "Wait a minute! I'm a good person, let me explain!" Do you call this low self-esteem? A person with low self-esteem would say, "I did this because I am a filthy sinner, and I deserve punishment." As a result, making excuses and low self-esteem contradict each other and cannot coexist.

The majority Christian psychology's tenants do not align with biblical teaching. For such a human-centric system, it is only natural to use highly equivocal language. The word "sin" has been replaced with all sorts of psychological terms. The lust of the flesh and the lust of the eyes and the boastful pride of life are now called "basic human needs." Natural consequences of someone's godless life are now termed "problems." Idolatry, in all its diversity, has been assigned the status of "human weaknesses" and "addictive behaviors." The list goes on.

So, the Book of Job is a great help in practical Christian life because it's focused on sin as the greatest problem of humankind. It teaches us to deal with sin first and foremost. When you read

God's words addressed to Job, a scary thought pops up in your head that God seems to have completely ignored the problem of pain and focused entirely on sin. He did not say a word about the horrors that befell the righteous man. He spoke to him as if nothing had happened. How shocking is that? From The Creator's speech, you don't really get the sense that He's talking to a sick, crushed, humiliated and bankrupted person with whom He was pleased. Think about how serious God's attitude must be towards human sin. He is not paralyzed by our pain and therefore can destroy sin. The more I reflect on how God spoke to Job, the more I appreciate their conversation. I understand more and more how important is was, in that particular moment, to help Job see his place before God and remind him of his rights and duties. From the point of view of Christian psychology, Job was a victim, and his tragedy was the ideal situation for reminding the poor sufferer of God's unfailing love. But he was comforted not by the overused and mushy "God loves you," but by the calm and authoritative "Hold your tongue!" In His stern rebuke, God subdued Job's rebellious heart.

> *Behold, I am insignificant; what can I reply to You?*
> *I lay my hand on my mouth.*
> *Once I have spoken, and I will not answer;*
> *even twice, and I will add nothing more.*
> *(Job 40:4–5)*

7

The Right of the Potter

The dispute between Job and his friends goes on for thirty-four chapters. The last one to speak was a certain Elihu, who is not mentioned either in the beginning or in the end of the book. He must have been completely ignored by Job, his three friends and God Himself. It is unclear when Elihu actually joined the conversation. We will not spend too much time analyzing his words for Job and his friends, because, in my opinion, he did not add anything new to the debate. Elihu was also mistaken about the nature of Job's tragedy, labelling it as God's corrective measure (33:19–30) and accusing the righteous man of every mortal sin (34:7–9, 35–37). He was clearly in the wrong when he made a statement about God not being affected by a man's righteousness or the lack of it. Wishing to emphasize the transcendence of the Creator with a view to condemning Job's desire to summon him to court, Elihu, like the previous speakers, overplayed his card in elevating God and humiliating man (35:6–8). On top of it all, he seemed to have had a very high opinion of his own theology, and, shall we say, did not suffer from a lack of self-esteem (36:3–4). To be sure, he said a lot of good things in his speech, and his last statements were simply admirable,

> "The Almighty—we cannot find Him. He is exalted in power and He will not do violence to justice and abundant righteousness. Therefore men fear Him; He does not regard any who are wise of heart." (37:23–24)

But let us leave Elihu for now. His personality is highly questionable in the context of the book, and unfortunately, we cannot get a clearer picture on who he was. In this chapter, I would like to pay closer attention to the main character and his words. The extended dispute between the four friends ends with God's monologue, which is not surprising. When truth comes, all lies disappear.

As I said in the previous chapter, the Lord appeared to Job in the storm, which probably means that He was angry. Note that in dealing with the prophet Elijah, who was gripped with fear, God spoke in a still small voice, but to the belligerent Job He came in a violent storm. Job did not actually *believe* that such a moment was possible. He did not think that God would actually stoop down and talk to him. "If I called and He answered me, I could not believe that He was listening to my voice . . ." (9:16). This had never happened before, but now the Creator himself appears on the stage. He did not send one of His angels. He did not speak to Job in his dreams, as Elihu suggested (33:14–16). He did not just drop a couple of phrases from Heaven. He came down himself and gave Job a very thorough reply. Can we do justice to the sheer beauty of this encounter? I think no one but Job could appreciate all the depth of what was happening. As for us, all we can do is extract valuable lessons out of this story in order to grow in our knowledge of God and godliness.

Oh, how Job dreamed of this moment, how he prayed and longed for it! "... Behold, here is my signature; let the Almighty answer me! And the indictment which my adversary has written" (31:35). His greatest desire was to *speak with God personally*. Not just in prayer as he had always done (one-sidedly), but face to face.

> "Oh that I knew where I might find Him, that I might come to His seat! I would present my case before Him And fill my mouth with arguments. I would learn the words which He would answer, and perceive what He would say to me." (23:3–5)

Job spent his whole life he faithfully praying to God. He believed God was hearing his prayers and answering them (12:4). He knew he didn't speak in vain. Most likely, God's answers came in the form of favorable circumstances and abundant blessings. At this time, however, he needed more than just speculations, guesswork, subjective interpretations or even dreams. He needed a *direct answer from God*. He needed it like air. He needed a dialogue, an opportunity to ask questions and get answers in a straightforward way, through physical senses, without the slightest hint of mystery. Job wanted the Creator to speak into his situation—he was primarily interested in learning God's heart. He was yearning to see God react in some way, to have him explain what was happening. He was dying to *see God face to face*.

There are plenty of people out there who know firsthand how empty the Heavens may feel in times of trouble. Everyone who has suffered knows very well the despair that settled in the silence of God, when your many prayers seem to have been wasted. When the going gets tough, Christianity seems like a complete joke. When your spiritual strength is gone, all you want to do is talk to God. We want to make sure that He is there for us, that He sees our tears and most importantly that He cares.

In any case, every single one of us at least once in our lifetimes wishes that we could get a personal note from God, so there wouldn't be any more doubts as to whether He spoke or not. When your faith wavers, it needs an encounter with God, because God is its only source of power. For the modern-day Christian, this encounter takes place daily in the pages of the Holy Scriptures. The truth of the Word of God nourishes our faith abundantly by strengthening and enriching it. I would be so happy if God appeared to me personally, but I know it probably won't happen. Knowing all my spiritual needs, God believes that the written Word is sufficient for me. It is the Word that reveals God to me and produces in me whatever is necessary for my sanctification. I am walking by faith, not by sight (2 Cor. 5:7).

Job, however, had no book to read in search of consolation. The Word of God could only come to him directly or through a prophet. In this case, the Lord chose the former, descending from Heaven to give him an answer. But do you know what brought the poor sufferer more comfort than hearing the words spoken by God? It was the simple fact that God took notice of him, and came down to speak to him personally even though he was a broken and suffering man.

I remember going through a very difficult time in my life and lifting up my eyes to the Lord day and night to pray for at least one little sign of His presence. I was asking God to send me an angel, give me a voice from heaven, or simply speed up His Second

Coming. But the heavens were empty and mockingly lifeless—with nothing happening. I kept begging, persevering in faith, but all in vain. The white clouds over my head were just floating away, totally indifferent to my misery. It seemed like God didn't care. I was never a mystic, so I wasn't expecting anything audible or visible that wasn't really there. After pouring out my heart to God, I concluded that there were only two possible explanations for this deafening silence: either there wasn't anybody up there, or it wasn't the right time for divine intervention in my life. As for me, I was sure that the time was ripe, but the Lord of Lords thought otherwise. I knew it perfectly well that it was useless to argue.

True, there are enough believers out there who would gladly convince themselves and others that God does in fact appear to them at such times. That He responds to them in an audible way, and that they, allegedly, spend hours and hours conversing with Him, asking questions, receiving answers, joking, sharing etc. The reality of God's silence must be so terrible, and their faith must be so weak that they would rather believe their fictional stories of God communicating with them in the same manner He did with Moses. Their rich imaginations are a way to compensate for the real spiritual hunger, and so they come up with all sorts of make-believe manifestations of the "supernatural." I don't judge them—I feel sorry for them. They reject God's right to decide for Himself how to communicate with people. He speaks to us on His own terms, and for our times He willed that Divine communication should primarily come to us in the form of the Holy Scriptures. Unfortunately, this is not the kind of communication that they look forward to or are able to accept. Their inner witness of the Spirit is so feeble (if at all present) that they need external evidence. Yet, those who are honest with themselves and ready to face reality head on, recognize that the times of extraordinary miracles are long past, revelations have ceased, and there is no point in pretending that nothing has changed since the time of the patriarchs or the apostles.[1]

In Job's case, he was probably sure that for the rest of his life he would be speaking into the void. Can you imagine what he must have felt like when the voice came to him out of the storm? He must have experienced both delight and horror at the same time—he was being spoken to by God Himself! The majestic Creator of the universe, who wields the absolute power over everything that exists, descended from His heavenly throne to speak with a humble and lowly man. God's monologue is very unique—it is the longest conversation between God and man recorded in Scripture in which God addresses one particular person. The Book of Isaiah may be huge, but in its pages God addresses various individuals. The same is true about the Book of Ezekiel or any other prophet. For example, Moses was a very prolific writer, but the words God spoke to him personally were few. Here we see God speaking to just one person, and it is a long discourse.

---

[1] As for me, I do believe in the relative possibility of personal revelations. It seems to me there is no evidence in Scripture that supernatural interventions have completely ceased. There can still be dreams, voices, visions, miracles, etc. However, there should be a very good reason for all of it. For example, I would be willing to believe in miracles in, for example, Muslim countries that do not have easy access to the Bible, which lead people to convert to Christianity—although every such testimony must be scrutinized against the Word of God. In Russia, where Bibles can be found in almost every bookstore and every home, the need for miracles is not so great. So, if I hear someone say they have had a supernatural experience—praise the Lord. But it is still someone else's spiritual experience, which is quite useless for my personal walk with God. Any personal spiritual supernatural experience is personal and therefore subjective, so we cannot apply it as something with universal and objective ramifications. Also, this does not mean that this person is somehow more "spiritual" or favored by God than people who do not have personal supernatural experiences, and such experiences are definitely not equal in authority to the Scriptures.

Chapter 7. The Right of the Potter

According to my calculations (based on the Russian translation), the Creator must have spoken for at least ten minutes. I wonder what Job was feeling when listening to the Lord of Lords for the whole ten minutes. I can vividly imagine the rolling thunder, the mighty gusts of wind and a lone weary man, barely standing on his feet. He is squinting through the clouds of dust, trembling and listening, unsure if he can trust his own ears. Out of the storm, words are coming to him in his own language with a distinct and unmistakable flavor—the words of God Himself, just for him. Frantic thoughts must have rushed through his mind: "He's heard me, He is answering, He cares for me, He is real!" He doesn't look very happy, but at least He is speaking. For a whole ten minutes there was no one else in the whole world except God and Job. Suddenly he could clearly see and feel that his life of self-imposed restrictions for God's sake and hardships which he endured to please Him, a life full of daily fights with the sinful flesh was not in vain! No! In the words of the psalmist—surely not in vain had he kept his heart pure and washed his hands in innocence (Ps. 73:13). All this time, the Creator was there, watching over him. Job had *believed* it in his heart, but now he *knew* it from his own experience. Here He is, He is near, and He cares. All grief, all despair, and all pain melted away before His face, whose seal of approval is worth more than all the troubles in the world. Who knows—Job may have been constantly repeating to himself, "Oh Lord, I hope I am not sleeping!"

He wasn't. The celestial drama reached its climax, when the main hero entered the stage. I remember reading the thirty-eighth chapter of the Book of Job for the first time. The more I read, the more I felt confused. Instead of answers and explanations which I expected to find, I counted about seventy questions asked by God. The whole monologue of the Creator is essentially one long question, and a rhetorical one at that. God's questions can be subdivided into three categories:

- Who are you?
- What do you know?
- What can you do?

From the very first sentence, the Lord chooses a strategy that can be called a "comparative analysis." In his complaints, Job was thinking a lot about God, but his focus was on his own righteousness, and on drawing a contrast between himself, his friends, and the wicked. Now it was time to show Job to whom he should have compared himself, and where his focus should have been. Generally speaking, the purpose of these questions was to explain to Job who he was in comparison to God:

- Nobody
- Knows little
- Can do even less

Who is This?

These are the first words addressed to Job. They mean, "Who are you?" God begins His discourse by pointing out the impassable chasm between the Creator and His creation. The rebuke of the Creator, begins with the reminder of who Job was in the created universe. To paraphrase, "First," says the Lord, "let us observe some subordination, so gird up your loins like a man and answer me. I see you have a serious charge against me. Before we look at it, let me ask you something." Then follows a long series of questions intended to help Job wake up to the reality of his present situation; he is a part of God's creation. Job belongs to God, as well as his deceased children, his lost estate, his servants, and the rest of creation—rivers, mountains, oceans, animals, etc.

Chapter 7. The Right of the Potter

> "Who has given to Me that I should repay him?
> Whatever is under the whole heaven is Mine." (41:11)

One of the key messages of the Book of Job is the sovereign reign of God (1:21). He is the Owner of the universe and has the right to do with His property whatever He wishes; He owes us nothing. When God takes something from us, He is taking what was already His! It is not injustice, theft or robbery. It is He who decides what to give and for how long. Our task is to properly accept the good gifts of the Most High, so that we can properly give them back—without tantrums, anger or grumbling. And most importantly, we should continue to worship and praise Him even when we give His good gifts back. There may be tears and pain of letting go, but we should remain humble in the awareness of our low position before the Almighty. For many people, being grateful in times of grief and loss would seem totally insane, a mockery of common sense. Such feelings and attitude are natural but wrong. Ingratitude is a fruit of the flesh (Rom. 7:18). Many people are thankful when they receive good gifts. Very few are thankful when they lose them. Become one of the few. Gratitude and praise are not only due when we have a "positive balance" in our account. And when it is negative, we don't need to pout or give God our "silent treatment". Ingratitude equals rejection of the sovereignty of the Creator, who has the right to do anything he wants with what belongs to Him.

God says to Job, "Look around: all of this is mine! What is the basis for your acting like an offended lender? You speak as though I violated some law. And, your words are so dead serious as though I was a defendant on trial! But who is it that I am talking to? Who are you? Are you so wise that you can teach me wisdom?" "You know, for you were born then, and the number of your days is great!" (38:21). The Lord resorts to sarcasm, which throws some healthy comedy into this drama. By this method

God helps Job to get rid of his habitual, earth bound, tragically grim view of his personal story. The Lord does not seem to care about Job being an unfortunate sufferer who lost his ten children in one day. He is not fixated on this at all. Instead, he is being ironic. The man is summoning God to court—that's funny and tragic at the same time!

One of the problems of Job as the indignant plaintiff was that he put too much trust in his own righteousness. An unrivaled spiritual giant, Job could not help but see how different he was from other people. Righteous in his own eyes, he believed that he was entitled to special treatment by God, which he had enjoyed for a number of years leading up to his misfortune. He saw his innocence as the basis for his entitlement. Job believed that he had a good chance to win the case, and so he readily filed his claim against God.

> "Behold now, I have prepared my case;
> I know that I will be vindicated." (13:18)

All that Job wanted to explain in the course of this trial was that the Creator had no right to act in this way, because he, Job, was a godly man, not a sinner (13:23). But didn't God know it already? Of course he did—after all, it was God who had declared Job righteous. Elsewhere in Scripture, God reaffirms his unique righteousness.

> "Then the word of the Lord came to me saying, 'Son of man, if a country sins against Me by committing unfaithfulness, and I stretch out My hand against it, destroy its supply of bread, send famine against it and cut off from it both man and beast, even though these three men, Noah, Daniel and Job were in its midst, by their own righteousness they could only deliver themselves,' declares the Lord God." (Ezek. 14:12–14)

"'Or if I should send a plague against that country and pour out My wrath in blood on it to cut off man and beast from it, even though Noah, Daniel and Job were in its midst, as I live,' declares the Lord God, 'they could not deliver either their son or their daughter. They would deliver only themselves by their righteousness.'" (Ezek. 14:19–20)

Note that Job is on God's list of the most respected saints of all time. Isn't it a straightforward confirmation of Job's unique status? Does it not entitle him to certain privileges? Technically, Job could have answered the question "Who is this?" by saying, "It's me, one of your best servants!" Maybe that's what Job was planning to say, but things turned out quite differently. Job did not realize that when you meet God face to face, all your complaints suddenly disappear, because imperfection cannot lay any claims to Perfection—only the reverse. For a human, meeting God is always a frightening experience, because suddenly you see a clear and overwhelming contrast between yourself and the Lord. When you encounter Him face-to-face, you realize that all your moral achievements and comparisons with other people are futile. In the light of the Absolute, the relative human dignity loses its glamor—the person becomes aware that the only reason God communicates with them is His pure grace. Mercy triumphs over merits.

The Book of Job conveys an uncomfortable but important message—God is free to do whatever He wishes with His creatures, just on the basis of being their Creator. In the third chapter, we already mentioned in passing that the potter has full rights over his clay. The Creator is above His creation! It was exactly what Job struggled with the most when he lamented not being able to file a lawsuit against God in any human institution. The Potter's right over His clay is an essential element of biblical theology, which is also mentioned in Isaiah, Jeremiah and Paul (Is. 29:16, 45:9, Jer. 18:6, Rom. 9). Of course, from the pot's point of view, this may seem like tyranny. But please bear with me as I quote the fitting words of Isaiah here, "Woe to the one who quarrels with his Maker—an earthenware vessel among the vessels of earth! Will the clay say to the potter, 'What are you doing?' Or the thing you are making say, 'He has no hands'?" (Is. 45:9).

Dear fellow pots (I refer to myself and everyone who's reading this now), allow me to give you a little speech. You can foam at the mouth in defending the rights of clay and stubbornly protesting against the injustice of bringing us down to the level of pots. This will not change anything. We will remain God's pots which He can use as He thinks fit. Job did nothing to deserve this nightmare. God simply willed that the righteous man should go through this. Why was it necessary? No explanation is given, praise the Lord! It would be really strange if the Potter had to give an account to His pottery. We tend to think too highly of ourselves. The Book of Job teaches us all an important message—a message from God. It goes something like this, "I'm the Potter, and you are pots. Humble yourselves!" Yet, there's no need to panic—our God is kind and loving. He has good plans for us, to give us a future and a hope (Jer. 29:11).

The Potter's right is the right of the Creator to override even the laws of sowing and reaping, on which the world is founded. Only He knows the reasons for what He does. "There is futility which is done on the earth, that is, there are righteous men to whom it happens according to the deeds of the wicked. On the other hand, there are evil men to whom it happens according to the deeds of the righteous. I say that this too is futility" (Eccl. 8:14). Don't criticize the Lord for not heeding the letter of the law—if He did, we would have all ended up in hell.

> "Then the Lord said to Job, 'Will the faultfinder contend with the Almighty? Let him who reproves God answer it.' Then Job answered the Lord and said, 'Behold, I am insignificant;

what can I reply to You? I lay my hand on my mouth. Once I have spoken, and I will not answer; even twice, and I will add nothing more.'" (40:1–5)

By the middle of the monologue, God calls Job to account, as if inviting him to join the conversation. And what do we see here—God's comparative analysis worked! The greatest of saints answers humbly, "Behold, I am insignificant; what can I reply to You? I lay my hand on my mouth" (40:4). First of all, Job realized that it was his complaints and protests that caused the Creator to react this way. He prudently put a hand on his mouth, refusing to speak any longer about the things he knew nothing about—"I lay my hand on my mouth." Let us also note how Job saw his self-esteem in light of what had happened—we discussed this topic in some length in the previous chapter. It is a very important achievement, considering how adamantly he protected his integrity.

I must say, it is a very healthy self-evaluation. It spares the person of all the grumbling against God, because it exposes his claims and protests as insults and ungratefulness. Such a self-evaluation helps us to realize that we have not deserved any of God's blessings. So, Job answered the first question of the Heavenly Counselor—who are you?—by calling himself insignificant.

God's Knowledge and Wisdom

"Who is this that darkens counsel by words without knowledge?" It seems to me that the best translation would be "Who is this that obscures Wisdom by words that do not contain knowledge?" The second rebuke of God was directed against Job's limited human knowledge. Job relied on his own in judging the Infinite and was disarmed by a series of questions, which showed God to be absolutely superior in wisdom.

> "Who set its measurements? Since you know. Or who stretched the line on it? On what were its bases sunk? Or who laid its cornerstone?" (38:5–6)
>
> "Have you understood the expanse of the earth? Tell Me, if you know all this. Where is the way to the dwelling of light? And darkness, where is its place, That you may take it to its territory and that you may discern the paths to its home?" (38:18–20)
>
> "Who has put wisdom in the innermost being or given understanding to the mind? Who can count the clouds by wisdom, or tip the water jars of the heavens, when the dust hardens into a mass and the clods stick together? (38:36–38)

Having exposed Job's intellectual deficiency, the Lord showed him that there was an unbridgeable intellectual gap between the Creator and his creation. Job does not have the slightest idea of the inner workings of the physical universe. The world is full of mystery. The incomprehensibility of God's nature is echoed in the incomprehensibility of the material universe. The inexplicable complexity and beauty of the world around Job is a hymn to God's creative power and wisdom—which our hero seemed to have forgotten.

Notice, God is not talking about spiritual things. Instead, He's touching upon such topics as earth, sky, night, day, lightning, thunder, clouds, snow, grass, desert, various animals, and birds. But what does creation have to do with Job's problem? Everything. The Creator consistently turns Job's attention to the manifold mysteries of the universe, which he took for granted. So, the Lord calls upon Job to examine Nature carefully and understand that the One who created such a complex, beautiful, interconnected, and orderly system deserves more trust than Job in his rebellion was willing to give him. A legitimate question is

> "Will the faultfinder contend with the Almighty?
> Let him who reproves God answer it." (40:2)

Chapter 7. The Right of the Potter

How often do we fall into temptation to "re-create" God in our image and likeness! How often do we attribute to Him our human qualities and traits! How hopelessly naive are our attempts to comprehend his intentions! The wisdom of God is unattainable for our finite human minds. Compared to God's mind, our minds are but amoeba's intellect. Our limited perception prevents us from even imagining the breadth and the depth of God's wisdom. However, this wisdom was in part reflected in the universe, as in a mirror. Its vast spaces stretching for trillions of light years, millions upon millions of galaxies, the mesmerizing beauty of the cosmos are but a trace, a glimpse into the heart of the Artist who crafted it all. Planet Earth is a complex system, every part of which sings praise to the Lord Almighty every second of the day.

Unfortunately, we tend to take too many things for granted. We perceive nature as the environment we need for our survival, which we can use for our own benefit. Yet, the world around us is much MORE than just habitat. The world is a hymn of praise sung to the Lord in words and notes of the created things. The world is our best helper in adoring the Lord. If you look at the world and give it some thought—God's presence is everywhere. Our finite minds are able to grasp at least some facets of his divine glory by studying the world through our five senses.

And when we enjoy the abundance around us, we essentially enjoy God's kindness. However, the enjoyment of any gift of God is incomplete and almost inappropriate if it does not lead to the recognition of the Giver. If I enjoy catching a perch in a pond but my delight does not extend to my relationship with the God who created the fish and gave it to me, then I am an unscrupulous consumer who neglects God's generosity. People seem to forget that they are not autonomous, but entirely dependent on the Creator. They are just too proud to admit it. Let's not forget that God's hand feeds us like all other creatures, including predators.

"Can you hunt the prey for the lion, or satisfy the appetite of the young lions, when they crouch in their dens and lie in wait in their lair? Who prepares for the raven its nourishment When its young cry to God and wander about without food?" (38:39–40)

The universe is the temple of the Creator. No architect will ever be able to build anything that would even remotely compare with its beauty and grandeur. No basilicas, no frescoes, no icons, no domes can create in my soul the same delight that I experience watching a sunset. No pillars, no ornaments, no murals, no moldings can make me sing to the Lord in the same way as I do while contemplating the vast array of stars at night. Oh, how pathetic are our human attempts to create something grandiose in order to inspire worship! When I play with my kitten, it inspires me to praise the Lord much more than all the majestic temples of the Middle Ages. Praise bursts out from my lips as I watch this graceful animal constantly "telling" me about my Lord. His movements, his jumps, his playfulness, his elegant walk, his color, his meowing, his purring, and thousands of other tricks communicate the message "Look at me and admire me. I am God's creation. I am a complex and beautiful being. Whoever made me is very intelligent and a connoisseur of beauty and aesthetics."

My enjoyment of God's gifts—gorgeous landscapes, delicious food, or fellowship with people—is much richer and much more fulfilling than that of an atheist. My ability to delight in creation always goes hand in hand with my delight in the Creator. A quiet morning yields me much more bliss than an atheist could ever have, because the gratitude that overflows in me is addressed to the right source, and does not rot in me like stagnant ditch water, poisoning my soul. My pleasures invariably lead me to praise God—and it should be that way. My delight in creation always

Chapter 7. The Right of the Potter

results in my enjoyment of the Creator! My pleasures are deep, meaningful and legitimate, and, therefore, full. I am functioning according to my design.

I am the image of God, the pinnacle of physical creation, and I allow all the other creatures of the world to perform the task of enriching my worship. Creation is always ready to pass the baton of praise to me, so that I, contemplating and admiring its manifold wisdom, would bask in the beauty of experiencing myself as part of it. I, as the pinnacle of creation, will give the much-deserved glory and praise to the Lord of Heaven. This will be the crown of our delight in earthly blessings. It's called worship! Oh, the joy of worship! Nothing can compare with it.

No, I will not be looking for an encounter with God among stones carved with a human hand. All the adornments of the most beautiful temples glorify MAN! And I want to worship God! As for me, I get distracted by the traces of excessive human activity. So, the flight of the bumblebee, the call of seagulls, the smell of flowers, the taste of my favorite fruit—all of this is the best context for my sincere worship, as well as its starting point. My prayers of thanks are most forced and unnatural when I am locked up within four walls. This is not to say that churches (buildings) are not necessary. All I want to emphasize is that we often do things out of habit, just because it's been done that way before. Someone may prefer worship in the building—praise the Lord. Buildings are comfortable and necessary. They have their purpose. I am speaking for myself—it is much easier for me to worship when I see the manifestations of God's glory all around me.

> "The heavens are telling of the glory of God;
> And their expanse is declaring the work of his hands.
> Day to day pours forth speech,
> And night to night reveals knowledge." (Ps. 19:1–2)

Nature is not silent. It is a herald of God's glory! The only reason we don't see or recognize the presence of God in the world around us is our total spiritual depravity. Only a madman could say that a penguin, a leopard, a peacock and hundreds upon thousands of other species of animals, birds and fish have been so beautifully adorned by some mindless nature. It's sheer insanity (Rom. 1:22)! And it is lawlessness to deprive the Creator of his glory. Divine retribution is upon us. God didn't leave us without some measure of knowledge of himself—his perfect attributes are imprinted in the splendor of the Universe.

> "Because that which is known about God is evident within them; for God made it evident to them. For since the creation of the world His invisible attributes, His eternal power and divine nature, have been clearly seen, being understood through what has been made, so that they are without excuse." (Rom. 1:19–20)

In some sense even a sparrow is God's messenger. He chirps, cleans his feathers, wallows happily in the mud, briskly hops off a branch at the sight of food, and fearlessly intruds into the company of pigeons, without any fear of being trampled. Watching him enjoy his sparrow life, I witness an incredible show staged by the best Producer. This sparrow is a miniature miracle, which is usually of interest only to cats (and their bias is understandable). The sparrow can't guess how much his existence causes me to give praise to our mutual Creator. When I am looking at him, I am positively sure that humans will never be able to re-create even the simplest of living cells—let alone such a funny bird. Even the "simplest" of cells is millions of times more complex than anything our human genius has come up with. God is above competition.

I have told you about the kitten and the sparrow. God questioned Job about the deer, the wild donkey, the horse, the rhinoceros, the peacock, the hawk, the eagle, and, lastly, about two other ancient creatures that we have difficulty identifying.[2] The righteous man received from the Master Designer a detailed description of the two most powerful animals in the ancient world. Speaking about the first one, God seems to have said, "Look how meticulously I have designed him. Look how beautiful he is, how well his body parts are joined together, how fearless and undaunted he is. It takes divine intellect to create something like this! "He is the first of the ways of God . . ." (40:19). One can say that God took Job to an imaginary planetarium, a botanical garden, or a zoo . . . And there you go—every single God's creature powerfully testifies about the Creator. Nothing reflects the wisdom of the Creator better than the created world. So when Job doubted God's wisdom, the Lord riveted his attention to the world around him and the creatures that fill it. Creation silences human ignorance. In his mind, Job believed in the wisdom of God and even preached about it (12:13).[3] It was the pressure of his dire circumstances that made him to slightly flinch where others would have been crushed. And so, when God himself addressed his doubts, he repented in ashes and answered the question: "What do you know?" in the following way,

> 'Who is this that hides counsel without knowledge?'
> "Therefore I have declared that
> which I did not understand,
> things too wonderful for me,
> which I did not know."
> (Job 42:3)

---

[2] Based on the description, God is here talking about some ancient animals (now extinct), most likely dinosaurs.

[3] See also Chapters 16 and 28.

8
The Right of the Potter (part 2)

God's Power and Sovereign Rule

God's absolute power and sovereignty is another important message of The Book of Job. The largest group of questions within the comparative analysis of the previous chapter deals with the *power* of the Creator versus the power of man. God establishes His infinite sovereignty over all creation. He reigns over:

- The cosmos (38:31–32);
- Forces of nature (38:33–38);
- The animal world (40:15);
- People (40:5–8);
- The spiritual realm (38:7–17).

Again, these questions were not asked to learn something new from Job; their purpose was to explain something to him. God already knew Job's spiritual, intellectual and physical limitations. After all, He is the Creator! God was after something else—His purpose was to communicate to, or rather, to remind Job of His infinite greatness. The Lord created the universe—this huge, complex, multi-level, and harmonious system which answers only to Him. He is the driving force behind all of its processes and its source of life. He is the beginning and the end. He sets the laws in motion by which the universe is governed. No one is able to fully grasp how the worlds were made, and therefore we should not interfere with God's wise decrees, much less accuse Him of making mistakes. Creation needs to be monitored all the time, and God watches over it day and night (Matt. 10:29–31). He commands the new day to arise (Job 38:12). He reigns by sending us rain, snow, sunshine, and wind in due time (38:22–30). He reigns by visiting the wicked with just retribution (38:12–15). He reigns by providing food to the living creatures, so they can have their young (39:1–4).

He is the Author of life. He created our consciousness, our ability to think, feel, invent, and thousands of complex and subtle emotions, talents and skills, and so much more. For us, our existence seems just natural. And we all crave to experience something supernatural. But if you think about it, life itself is a miracle. People walk, sleep, eat, see, hear, think, but are totally unaware of how these "natural processes" are connected with the Creator. Too bad! "In whose hand is the life of every living thing, and the breath of all mankind?" (12:10). It is He who commands our hearts to beat, our blood to run through the arteries and veins, our eyes to see and ears to hear. It is through His power that food is digested in our stomachs and hair grows on our heads. It was He who invented thousands of biochemical reactions in our bodies and makes sure that they run smoothly. The cells are

Chapter 8. The Right of the Potter (part 2)

dividing at his bidding. He speaks, and life starts forming in the womb of the mother.

People often say without giving it a second thought, "I am grateful to my parents for giving me life." What blasphemy! These words may seem beautiful and heartfelt, but in reality, they are nothing but beautified idolatry. There's no more intellect involved in this process than in the pairing of two monkeys. Later on it gets more interesting. When a woman gets pregnant, at first, she doesn't even know about it. It may be a whole month before she realizes that she "gave" life to someone. For fathers it is usually a lot longer. They simply can't guess whether the "child-creating act" was successful. They are usually informed later, and they are often surprised at the news even though they were so eager to share their lives with someone. Often these "life-givers" (both men and women) would do anything to avoid pregnancy. Strangely enough, some couples cannot help getting pregnant, while others have a hard time conceiving. In short, our control over the process of giving life is quite negligible.

So, when a woman finds herself pregnant, her participation in the process of "creating" the child is virtually nonexistent. All she does is eat, sleep, grow sideways, and look at herself in the mirror more often. Her belly grows by itself—she is not even involved in the process. Have you ever seen a pregnant woman sitting in an armchair, clasping her hands, biting her lips, and "forcing" her fetus to form inside her body? I think not. She is not the one to choose the color of her baby's hair and eyes, nor does she sculpt his or her nose, and certainly she does not determine the gender. All of this the mother finds out much later. She just goes on living. The only difference is that now she takes better care of herself. Meanwhile, someone's invisible hand molds and shapes the little body inside her womb performing such complex tasks which we cannot even begin to imagine. We can only describe them in vague terms (Ps. 139:13; Job 10:8–11). The doctors provide the parents with the most general information about what and when is being formed in a child. The parents, however, have no idea about what is actually happening. This is how we "give" life to others!

People tend to easily forget their limitations. It is not surprising that most of God's questions for Job seem to address the scope of his abilities. They often start with the "can you?"

> "Can you bind the chains of the Pleiades, or loose the cords of Orion? Can you lead forth a constellation in its season, and guide the Bear with her satellites? Do you know the ordinances of the heavens, or fix their rule over the earth? Can you lift up your voice to the clouds, so that an abundance of water will cover you? Can you send forth lightnings that they may go and say to you, 'Here we are?'" (38:31–35)

> "Can you bind the wild ox in a furrow with ropes,
> or will he harrow the valleys after you?" (39:10)

> "Do you make him leap like the locust?
> His majestic snorting is terrible." (39:20)

> "Behold, I am insignificant; what can I reply to You?
> I lay my hand on my mouth." (40:4)

> "Can you draw out Leviathan with a fishhook?
> Or press down his tongue with a cord?" (41:1)

Doesn't it sound strange? What was the purpose behind this weird demonstration of power to a mortal man who was in deathly agony? How could this "reminder" of God's physical supremacy comfort the poor soul? What was the point of describing a ferocious dinosaur to Job in such meticulous detail? Does this beast have anything to do with anything? Does it really have a connection to Job's perished children? Let's find out.

Behemoth and Leviathan

The description of the two most powerful (at least at that time) beasts created by God takes up about forty percent of God's speech. God uses them to illustrate his infinite greatness. Behemoth is called "the first of the ways of God." No one can kill him except God Himself. Leviathan is proclaimed "king over all the sons of pride" (41:34). He was invincible and did not know fear (41:33). His "combat qualities" made him superior to all other representatives of the animal kingdom. These two creatures were virtually unconquerable, and did not answer to the so-called "kings of nature." The earth was originally given to man for management, but there was this sharp-toothed monster in their sphere of influence, which could not be subdued. The "Behemoth" and the Leviathan had only one master—God Himself! The Creator seemed to say, "See these beasts? They are the work of my hands. You can do nothing with them, but I can! They are in my power, and so are you. I am the Master. Stop this competition with me once and for all."

> "Will you really annul My judgment? Will you condemn Me that you may be justified? Or do you have an arm like God, and can you thunder with a voice like His? Adorn yourself with eminence and dignity, and clothe yourself with honor and majesty. Pour out the overflowings of your anger, and look on everyone who is proud, and make him low. Look on everyone who is proud, and humble him, and tread down the wicked where they stand. Hide them in the dust together; bind them in the hidden place. Then I will also confess to you, that your own right hand can save you." (40:8–14)

In this one sentence the Lords reveals the root cause of Job's complaints (v. 8). Job is accusing the Almighty of acting *unjustly towards his creation*. And this is not just about Job. It's about the whole world. Job sees himself as just one victim of this global injustice, perpetrated by the Creator. Also notice the connection between verses eight and nine; there isn't any. Some connection is certainly there, but it is a very strange one, unexpected and scary to be sure. I was expecting to hear anything from God in verse nine, but not this. It would have been reasonable for the Lord to start instructing Job, following his accusations, about his intellectual bankruptcy and inability to see through all circumstances. It would have been understandable if the Lord just pointed out to Job that God's purpose was to check whether His righteousness had anything to do with personal gain. It would have been understandable if the Lord simply insisted that He was just, and that there was an explanation for everything. And finally, it would have been understandable if the Lord promised to Job that this tragedy would ultimately work for his good. But what about this "display of power" in verses 9–14? Why would God refer to His infinite power in response to the Job's charges laid at the door of heavenly justice? What is the logic behind it? This is so similar to a street fight when two boys of different ages and sizes argue about something:

"That's not fair! Give me my ball!"

"How about a punch in the eye instead?"

Let me translate verses 9 through 14 into the language of a street fight, though with softer terms, "You say it's unfair for me to take your ball? But don't you see that I'm the strongest one in the neighborhood? Look at how tall I am and how big my muscles are. I can take all the balls in the neighborhood and beat up everyone. And no one can beat me. Can you do the same? Nope! Come back when you can, and I will be your friend." *That's the essence of what God said to Job.* How does that sound to you? Can you hear that without cringing? If in the course of your Christian life you have not developed a nasty habit of turning to double standards whenever you are confronted with difficult or uncomfortable passage in Scripture, then you are probably going to be perplexed with this one. For many years, the Book of Job left me perplexed. I could not see any satisfactory logical links between the above-stated argument and the corresponding counter argument.

And do you know what prevented me from seeing those links? My own theology! It was infected by the poison of a man-centered worldview, and so the gap between me and God was artificially narrowed. In theory, I knew that he was the sovereign Creator over all things, but I refused to see that this sovereignty extended to his children as well. I chose to believe that he was very limited in how much he could actually bring upon his faithful servants. "No, no," I used to say, "God needs a *good reason* to act sternly towards His own. If a Christian is suffering, he must have done something wrong. "Wait a minute," I said in the next breath, "but Job didn't do anything wrong. So, why did God do such a thing to a righteous man?" "Well, maybe Job wasn't *totally sinless,*" I kept insisting. "And this must have been a lawful reason for God to give him trouble."

> "Yet these things You have concealed in Your heart;
> I know that this is within You:
> If I sin, then You would take note of me,
> And would not acquit me of my guilt." (10:13–14)

Later, however, I realized that even Jesus, who was absolutely sinless, was subjected to the kind of suffering that Job could not even imagine. It means that those who find themselves on God's anvil do not necessary deserve it. I had to stop seeking for a comfortable solution. Tearfully I accepted the fact that God must have the right to inflict pain even on those who love Him, simply because He is God!

Dear reader, please don't be alarmed—don't allow your fear to make you want to justify God's actions. Don't say "Because God never acts without a purpose, there must be some plan in letting me go through all these troubles. He must have been after my happiness, although I don't know what kind of happiness it is." There is a clear danger here of a man-centered approach, which interprets God's sovereign actions as always aimed at our well-being. Let's not forget that all His actions are aimed, first and foremost, at exalting His own glory (Prov. 16:4; Is. 48:9–11; Ezek. 36:20–23). We tend to cling to "all things work together for our good," and this is correct (Rom. 8:28). But we have to understand what is primary and what is secondary. Our spiritual good, which is often the result of going through difficulties, is a side effect of God's commitment to His own glory. We should not only be comforted by the knowledge that all our troubles lead to some good end, but also by the fact that God is *glorified* through them.

"Yet, there must be something," I repeatedly said to myself, "that holds God in check. There must be some law that he and I equally observe. There must be a set of rules that *we both* adhere to. Then I could potentially stick my finger in a contractual clause or article, and call Him to account." And then suddenly I realized I was speaking like Job, lamenting like Job, and dreaming like Job.

> "For He is not a man as I am that I may answer Him, that we may go to court together. There is no umpire between us, who may lay his hand upon us both." (9:32–33)

There is no mediator between God and me, there is no third party to call God to account for His actions. And there is no law under which I, a citizen of Heaven, could challenge God's actions because of something He "did wrong." "But how about the moral principles He Himself laid down?" I continued my ruminations.

Chapter 8. The Right of the Potter (part 2)

"God is holy, He cannot sin. So, is He actually limited in any way?" Well, yes and no. We operate at different levels; He is the Potter, and I am a pot. Here's what I mean. I can't just decide to take somebody's life. It would be a sin. But it is only a sin for me, a mortal man.

Scripture clearly teaches that God can put people to death and inflict punishment on many, including women and children (1 Sam. 15:1–3; 2 Kings 2:24). For me deception is a sin, but God can intentionally misinform people while pursuing his own purposes (1 Kings 22:20–23; Ex. 3:16–18). I cannot judge others, but God can (Jam. 4:12). By acting this way, He is not compromising His holiness. He has the rights of the Potter.

> "Then I went down to the potter's house, and there he was, making something on the wheel. But the vessel that he was making of clay was spoiled in the hand of the potter; so he remade it into another vessel, as it pleased the potter to make. Then the word of the Lord came to me saying, 'Can I not, O house of Israel, deal with you as this potter does?' declares the Lord. 'Behold, like the clay in the potter's hand, so are you in My hand, O house of Israel.'" (Jer. 18:3–6)

I remember getting very excited when I first discovered that the Lord was calling me His friend and Himself my Father. Immediately His lordship and sovereignty began to fade away in my mind, for some reason. I quickly realized that being God's friend and son had clear advantages over the whole idea of Him being the sovereign ruler—I assumed I had the rights and privileges of a son. However, I overlooked the fact that in Scripture, only one privilege of a friend is mentioned, namely, more awareness, a deeper spiritual knowledge. "No longer do I call you slaves, for the slave does not know what his master is doing; but I have called you friends, for all things that I have heard from My Father I have made known to you" (John 15:15).

Unfortunately, we misunderstand His desire to bring us closer to Himself. We seem to always go from one extreme to the other, and away from the happy medium.[1] He is not the kind of friend that we tend to imagine—according to the flesh. He really wants to be our friend, but He has His conditions. In the Gospel of John, one verse earlier, we see Jesus granting the disciples a privilege and then pointing out their part of the deal—the condition. "You are My friends if you do what I command you" (John 15:14). It was precisely this clause that I mysteriously overlooked for a long time (and I am not alone). I wanted His friendship, but according to my idea of friendship. It's also important to note that this is the only passage representing the Lord as our friend. This means that the frequency of our using this epithet should be relatively low. In all other cases, we are dealing with the King of Kings and the Lord of Lords. We should not forget that.

But let's go back to God's sovereign reign. By stressing again the extent of His power, the Lord forcefully asserts his absolute sovereignty. Supremacy in power is just one of the components of the "Potter's law". God is above His creatures in power, and it is part and parcel of His intellectual and moral superiority. The Potter is above His pottery!

Beginning with the 40th chapter, the Lord starts talking about this power specifically in the context of destroying the high and mighty of this world (v. 6–8). He challenges Job with a direct question (my own paraphrase): "Can you exterminate all evil from the face of the earth?" The answer is obvious—no. Only God is able to bring down all the haughty and destroy all the wicked. Only God is strong enough to protect us against evil. He did so for Job for so many years, and Job was able to enjoy a season of peace. God hedged him in by putting a wall of safety

---

[1]Some people lack reverence and awe; they act as if the Lord was their buddy. Others lack intimacy and passion; they believe God is a policeman whose only goal is to enforce the law.

Chapter 8. The Right of the Potter (part 2)

all around him. It was God's hand that was guarding Job from trouble, while Job was clueless about what was happening. God provided Job with this little paradise on this accursed earth, even though *He didn't have to do it.* The Lord's answer becomes very clear in light of the statements Job made earlier. Here is our hero's opinion on God's relative success in limiting evil in the world:

> "It is all one; therefore I say, 'He destroys the guiltless and the wicked.' If the scourge kills suddenly, He mocks the despair of the innocent. The earth is given into the hand of the wicked; He covers the faces of its judges. If it is not He, then who is it?" (9:22–24)
>
> "From the city men groan, and the souls of the wounded cry out; yet God does not pay attention to folly." (24:12)

Not a very flattering assessment, don't you think? Then Job shared how he himself was fighting with evil:

> "I put on righteousness, and it clothed me;
> My justice was like a robe and a turban." (29:14)
>
> "I broke the jaws of the wicked
> And snatched the prey from his teeth." (29:17)

What a champion for justice! What a role model! Turns out the Lord wasn't doing a good job punishing evil. Job was much better at it. It is also interesting that even though Job doubted God's desire to restore the righteous and destroy the wicked, he never questioned God's power to do so. Chapter 12 is a hymn to God's sovereignty. In it, we see Job's unflinching faith in God's total control over everything that happens. He knew very well about the wisdom and the power of the Creator. "With Him are strength and sound wisdom" (12:16). Job also knew very well the eternal destiny of sinners. In chapter 27 he makes a statement that though God may allow the lawless to prosper on earth for a short time, their prosperity is fleeting and shaky. So even before meeting God face to face, Job was well-versed in theology. So, what's the deal here? What was the source of all these accusations, and where did the desire to sue the Lord come from?

Life is a territory where theory and practice often clash. We tend to know much more than we practice. So, the problem is often not a lack of knowledge but a lack of determination to act accordingly. For this reason, *reminding* someone again and again of something they already know seems like a good idea. "Therefore, I will always be ready to remind you of these things, even though you already know them, and have been established in the truth which is present with you" (2 Pet. 1:12; see also 1 Cor. 15:1; 2 Tim. 2:14; Tit. 3:1). We cannot help seeing the discrepancy between our words and actions. The important thing here is not to get stuck in a rut. It is much worse when believers *separate* theory from practice. Unfortunately, I have heard many people claim, "The Bible says is one thing, but life is a totally different matter." This phrase usually means, "You may preach whatever you want, but life is always more complicated than that. Life is full of situations which the Bible does not address. Thank you for the beautiful fairy-tales, but we have to live in the real world."

Are there really areas where theological theory and practice never intersect? I don't believe so. Jesus was able to put the two together perfectly well. The real problem is not in the seeming lack of practicality of the Word of God, which is, allegedly, not applicable to our modern times. The problem is the inability of the vast number of believers to embrace the high price of obeying God's will. They justify their unwillingness to make sacrifices for the sake of the Lord—give up their earthly safety, time, health, comfort, money etc.—by referring to their "unique" circumstances, not accounted for by the "theory." In reality, however, there is no special life context in which the Word of God would be irrelevant. Yet, some Christians love their lives so much that they are not ready to serve God regardless of the cost. They would rather make excuses. Even a minor hardship or persecution is too much to endure (Phil. 2:8). That's what the problem is.

However, none of this applies to Job. Let me repeat, he only slightly flinched where others would have collapsed. All he needed to do was to take the focus off of himself, his problems, his pain, and fix his gaze upon God. He needed a powerful reminder that he was not the center of the universe, but only a small fraction of it. He needed to come to grips with his total helplessness and total dependence on the Almighty, both in time of prosperity and trouble. When he was saving the destitute, he did so with God's permission and with God's resources. In a fit of temper, he blamed the Almighty for having too weak a desire to bring order on earth, all the while it was God who was breaking the jaws of the wicked through Job. Without Him, Job would not have accomplished much. Without the King of Kings, he wouldn't have saved anybody, including himself.

> "Hide them in the dust together; bind them in the hidden place. Then I will also confess to you, that your own right hand can save you." (40:13–14)

God seems to be saying, "I have been in the justice business for so long. Sorry, I didn't see you joining in. There's one little problem—*you are totally helpless*. I've heard you boast about how you punish the bad guys and rescue the good guys. You make it sound like I should have been learning from you. I must have gotten too lazy here in Heaven, and didn't notice atheists taking over the world. Sorry, I've neglected my duties." And then Lord pointed out to Job that it's not a creature's role to explain the Creator how to utilize His power. "Will the faultfinder contend with the Almighty?" (40:2).

But didn't Job know he could not contend with the Almighty? Didn't he know that God was the Ruler of the universe? Of course, he did. But let's see how much regret Job felt right after embracing the idea of God's sovereignty:

> "But He is unique and who can turn Him? And what His soul desires, that He does. For He performs what is appointed for me, and many such decrees are with Him. Therefore, I would be dismayed at His presence; when I consider, I am terrified of Him. It is God who has made my heart faint, and the Almighty who has dismayed me, But I am not silenced by the darkness, nor deep gloom which covers me." (23:13–17)

Now everything was different. Now he was speaking without bitterness, but with delight, which was the overflow of a humble heart.

> "I know that You can do all things, and that no purpose of Yours can be thwarted. 'Who is this that hides counsel without knowledge?' Therefore I have declared that which I did not understand, things too wonderful for me, which I did not know. 'Hear, now, and I will speak; I will ask You, and You instruct me.' I have heard of You by the hearing of the ear; but now my eye sees You; therefore I retract, and I repent in dust and ashes." (42:2–6)

Breaking Free

For Job it was a giant spiritual leap. It was not so much a leap in terms of gaining knowledge as it was a leap in character formation. He received personal revelation, and suddenly his sufferings were not meaningless. Things started making sense not because Job was finally able to grasp God's ultimate purpose for this tragedy, but because he embraced them as something that came from God. He *humbled himself*. He saw the Master of the universe with his own eyes.² The Heavenly Counselor enlightened his situation by giving him a totally new plane of reference, without which all our misfortunes would seem hopeless and dark. This reference point was God Himself. God's presence changes everything. Any hardship will loosen its grip on you the moment you allow God into the circumstance. Things will change, even if you have no answers. Answers don't really help—they *cannot give comfort* to the suffering soul. Only God can truly comfort. Without Him, you can only endure your troubles, wait them out, bury them in the sands of time, but you can never get comforted overnight. However, when God enters the scene, everything that seemed hopeless and unbearable suddenly is perceived in a different light. Job no longer needed God's answers to the question "Why?" C. S. Lewis once poignantly said about God: "You are the answer." God is the answer to any grief and pain. When truth comes, our subjective feelings recede into the background. Truth really sets you free.

The very moment the Creator appeared before Job and began to speak, the world around Job changed once and for all. It changed at the level of perception. It was no longer a meaningless three dimensional world. It acquired a new dimension. In the gusts of the strong wind, Job felt the breath of eternity, before which all temporary earthly troubles faded away. Everything was different. There was a new way to look at losses, friends, merits, life, death, the past, and future. The presence of God brought him a very keen awareness of the fleeting nature of our earthly existence. The burden of earthly pain and loss was lifted. In times of illness and infirmity, we become aware of our own frailty, but when we come to grips with the eternal, this awareness is doubled.

---

²What I mean is that Job saw certain *physical* appearances (we can only guess what they were) which contributed to his personal revelation. No one has seen God at any time (John 1:18).

At that moment, Job *experienced* something he always *knew* in theory; our earthly life is but a step, over which eternity tripped and continued on its way. This life on earth is not the end but the beginning.

Job could no longer long for death, as he had the day before. Life has meaning under any circumstances, when its main component is God. Life is worth living, because nothing terrible has actually happened. The most terrible thing is to never have known God. The most terrible thing is to be rejected by Him. The most terrible thing is to be in Job's situation and have God as an enemy. Job knew very well that he "belonged to Heaven." He was acutely aware of it, despite God's apparent sternness. He was deeply assured of God's acceptance, because he had strong faith, he was thirsting for righteousness, and he received a very specific personal revelation. Now he knew his trials weren't punishment; they weren't the consequence of some past sin. His suffering wasn't a sign of rejection or some rift in their relationship. What a relief it was! It's my God, my kind and just Master. Job's despair was lifted in an instant because despair is always the result of distorted thinking, and the presence of God destroys all lies. He received no answers as to the causes of the tragedy or possible benefits it was going to produce. He was still poor and ill, but he was comforted by the presence of God.

Many of us live in constant fear of the future, because we are aware of the unpredictability of God's ways. We pray, attend church regularly, do good . . . and hope to avoid trouble. We tremble at the very thought of being in Job's situation, because we can only see how he suffered and nothing else. Like Peter, we are gripped by the fear of loss and physical pain, and do not want to set our gaze on the life to come. We are not interested in even considering the blessings that could come to us or someone else as a result of our suffering. All we want is to keep all unpredictable circumstances at bay.

Chapter 8. The Right of the Potter (part 2)

I remember very well how angry I was while reading and rereading the story of Joseph, the son of Jacob. I was really appalled by the explanation Joseph gave to his ordeals at the end of the story. "Now do not be grieved or angry with yourselves, because you sold me here, for God sent me before you to preserve life" (Gen. 45:5). "But Joseph said to them, "Do not be afraid, for am I in God's place? As for you, you meant evil against me, but God meant it for good in order to bring about this present result, to preserve many people alive" (Gen. 50:19–20). "What sort of explanation is this?" I fulminated in my rage. What does this "do not be grieved or angry with yourselves" mean? Joseph's logic was beyond me! When I put myself in his shoes, I couldn't help feeling outraged, "But this is my life! Mine!" I didn't choose such a monstrous self-sacrifice! I wasn't even asked! Why do I have to be a slave, spend the best years of my life in prison and endure so much just for the sake of a bunch of people who were starving? Why me? You are God Almighty! I am sure you could have found a way to avoid such a sacrifice on my part! Thank you. This "Egypt test" is not for me. I don't need the riches and power. Just give me a normal life." But unlike me, Joseph did not consider his life as his own. He humbled himself before God. He feared sinning against Him more than pain and suffering. That's why, he is one of my favorite Bible heroes (along with two others).

I want to describe here a hypothetical situation to illustrate how tightly bound we are to the earth. Imagine for a moment that you are Job. One day, the Lord appears to you and says, "I offer you two choices for how you can spend your life. Option one: in a couple of days, all of your ten children will die, you will lose all your possessions, get a terrible skin disease, and, on top of that, all your relatives and friends will turn away from you. But in return, your life story will become part of the Word of God, the whole world will know you, millions of people will get encouraged through your example, you will help me win the argument with Satan, you will make a giant leap in your spiritual growth and receive a special reward in eternity. And one more thing: after you have had your fill of suffering, I will give you other children and a double portion of whatever you have lost. Option two: nothing changes, and you live on quietly till you die."

I can probably guess what you would have chosen, and I will tell you what my choice would have been. I would have readily said something like this to the Lord, as respectfully as I could, "Thank you, Lord, but I don't want any changes! And I don't need fame or wealth. I can't complain about my spiritual growth either. Also, I do not want to encourage others at the cost of losing my own children, and so, I will humbly forego the honor of being incorporated into the list of Bible heroes. Please do not be angry, but I do not wish to prove anything to Satan and do not want to be part of your prehistoric argument. Moreover, I am quite ready to give up my health, all my money, and my life itself in order to save my children. Please let my children live. Why would you even care about what this man-hater thinks? Just let me continue enjoying my happiness. *I am perfectly happy.*"

If you tell me that you would have chosen the first option, I will not believe you. But do not worry—this choice will never be offered to any of us. It is Providence and the exclusive right of the Lord of Lords to come up with dilemmas and solutions. I just wanted to show that the first option has nothing naturally appealing to us. We cling to our small joys. We ask God to help us along in our affairs—give protection, provision, guidance, blessing, etc. For us happiness is this perfect life where everything goes the way we want. In our scenario, God gets the role of the Fulfiller of our desires; therefore, there are quite a few people out there who would just add God to their lives, because such an addition can translate into great advantages. And why not? Is it so bad to be under the protection of the most powerful being in the universe?

But the Creator will not accept the role of a free addition to the already established life values, desires, and patterns. He wants to become the highest value in our lives, the chief desire of our hearts, and, above all, our life itself. God is the only One who is worthy of such a status. To reach this goal, He is ready to take us through pain, darkness, despair and tears if necessary. He knows there's nothing more important than our personal communion with Him. We, believers, understand this too... but in theory. On a day-to-day basis, however, we live in fear. There is a simple reason for this—we have not yet died for ourselves. We have a constant fear that God might take away whatever joy we have or withhold something we really want. For us, it's a kind of lottery—we never know if we will get what we want. With this perspective, we do not value our relationship with God. We only value what we can cajole out of him. As a result, worship becomes conditional and dry. We have no intimacy with God.

There has always been and there will always be an interesting and quite a large category of "believers" who are sort of stuck between two opposite realities. They are already strangers to the world, and it is scary for them, but Christ also seems too far away. Prayer, worship, Bible reading are but duties to be performed. Their hearts are bound to earthly, mundane things, which seem to bring them genuine joy. They trust God to a certain degree, but have a death grip on this temporary life. They want to live as comfortably as they can, preferably without trouble, and then go to heaven after death. Yet, the following three components make their lives unbearable: (1) strong desires that can only be satisfied in this life; (2) the unstable and dangerous world which entices you to pay a huge price for satisfying these desires; (3) the uncontrollable and unpredictable God who seems to be too focused on our spiritual growth instead of simply giving us all we want, bail us out of trouble and rescue from all danger. With such an unavoidable combination, there's only one thing left—life in constant fear.

Unlike his wife, Job did not live for earthly pleasures, yet he was afraid of losing his blessings, which is of course quite natural. At first, he did not even want to part with the privileges he was given, without a good enough reason. But the Lord decided to help him put into practice this perfectly correct theory of loss. By doing this, God must have forever saved Job from the fear of losing earthly things. With this giant leap in spiritual growth, Job obtained a new dimension of freedom. All of the crutches were knocked out from underneath him, and there was only support left—God! If there were any cords that bound him to this earth before his suffering, they were now gone. Everything was lost, but life was going on! That's why the last words of Job are the words of penitence. The "pot" stopped grumbling and rebelling, and with humility and trust gave himself up into the hands of the Potter.

> *I have heard of You by the hearing of the ear;*
> *but now my eye sees You;*
> *therefore I retract,*
> *and I repent in dust and ashes.*
> *(Job 42:5–6)*

9
THE MEANING OF LIFE

There comes a time when every person starts reflecting on the meaning of life—where he came from, where he is going, what will happen after death. Such reflections are common for those who bear God's image. Yet, the mind of an average person will at best just scratch the surface, without delving into the full depth of the issue. Similarly, a small child will just peep through the door of a mysterious chamber, only to jump back in fear of what might happen next. Whatever is behind that door is scary. There is a totally different reality out there, the echoes of which reverberate in our world through our disturbed conscience. It may hold hidden answers to the most challenging questions with which human minds inevitably wrestle. So, what's the deal? Let's get on with it! Don't you want to know who you are, where you came from, and what you are here for? Well, not so fast. It's quite intriguing that people actually *do not want* to know. Even after some contact with the truth, which indeed can set you free from the abyss of ignorance, we still turn away.

They might feel compelled to pay a little tribute to their intellectual and moral self-image by saying through a yawn, "What is truth, after all?"—while making it clear to you that you can keep your answer to yourself (John 18:38). And if you still give it to them, they may go as far as covering their ears and giving you some trouble (Acts 7:57). The truth hurts, and elicits one of two reactions: submission or rejection. Rejection may vary from fierce malice to superficial compromise (Luke 8:11–18).

You see, human life is inextricably linked to the idea of God's existence, but we still run away from God (Gen. 3:8; Rom. 3:11). Every time our meandering carnal mind is confronted with the truth, it gets scared and shuts down. Just hearing the word "God" casually dropped in a conversation, will immediately shrink up the mind of an unbeliever to the degree that it will start scurrying around like a cockroach caught off guard on a kitchen table. Quick, quick, quick—back into the crack, away from the light. By reminding people of God, you lead them by the hand to that very door, to which they have been before, perhaps may have even tried to open more than once. But they don't really want to enter. They despise the very idea of going through, leaving their familiar world behind. They are afraid to break out of the confines of their pseudo-reality, where everything is comfortable and predictable: home, work, family, sleep . . . and my "innocent" sinful pleasures. Like a magpie, they will stuff up their minds with all kinds of shiny objects, so as not to be left alone with the troubling thoughts about the Omniscient. They will give their full attention to a created thing—anything from insects to stars—but they will not be genuinely interested in the One who created the insects and stars. In short, our human minds will happily engage in anything except God.

But what is behind that door, what is so scary? Why would a guy sitting next to you on a plane carefully listen to you as you ramble away on quantum physics, which he doesn't understand, but immediately shut down and start nervously twitching as soon as you utter the trigger word "God?" Why, after having such a good time for so long, he basically asks you to end the conversation? You see, the very idea of God's existence grabs a man by the scruff of his neck and pulls him from under the bed where he is hiding like a mischievous cat who made a puddle in the wrong place. The very mention of God pokes him right back into . . . the stinking reality of his sinful life. People are often uncomfortable or embarrassed by the very mention of God, because it brings up their guilt! Not the guilt that pings a child who stole some money out of his mom's purse, but a deep existential guilt, arising from the very core of our being and is inseparable from our self-awareness. It is not so much a consequence of a person's understanding that he's not what he should be, but rather a consequence of knowing that he's *not willing* to change anything! That's what tightens its grip! So what do we do? Do we hastily run to the water and wash off the dirt as soon as a ray of sunlight exposes our filthy existence? Not at all. We back away into the darkness so as not to see our own filth. Don't we want to come to Him who can cleanse us from all unrighteousness (1 John 1:9)? No, we don't! We are satisfied with the status quo, and *this* is exactly what causes us to flee from the light. They *love* darkness, even though they know that it's wrong (John 3:19–20). That's where the guilt is coming from.

Therefore, all questions related to our existence are moral rather than intellectual in nature. Answers to these questions force us to change, give up something, impose restrictions on ourselves. That's why the majority of people don't even bother to open this mysterious door. They take their earthly existence for granted. They don't look for any philosophical explanations for the purpose of life, they just exist. They live as if they were eternal.

What madness! Even a pig led to the slaughter will kick and squeal—it feels its impending doom. A man, however, will march to his death with a resolute face, ignoring the warnings of his half-strangled conscience. This is a feast during the plague. This is a dance on board the Titanic. This is free falling . . . without a parachute. We *know* we have to give an account for everything we have done, but our love of sin prevails over our common sense (Rom. 1:32).

My cat (sorry for another cat example) is not concerned about why I feed him, where his food comes from, why he has a place to sleep, why I scratch him behind his ears and play with him every day. Even so, his expression never reveals anything even remotely resembling a concern for the meaning of life. He takes everything for granted. But he is a cat. He is not supposed to ask questions. However, he doesn't ignore my presence. He is glad to see me enter through the door. He rubs against my feet and shows some signs of attachment. He acknowledges me as his Master, as well as the fact that he gets his food out of my hands—and an occasional spanking.

People, however, will readily consume whatever Lord gives (just like my cat), but will pretend that their Master does not exist (Is. 1:3). They believe themselves to be the only source of good things in life and try to "enjoy it to the fullest." They shut down any disturbing thoughts about life being much more than eating, drinking, wearing beautiful clothes, working, getting married, raising children or having fun. I have an acquaintance, a non-believer, who *doesn't even allow* me to mention God, the meaning of life, the imminence of death, or anything "supernatural." He just says, "I am terrified by these conversations. Please stop!" What do you think about an answer like that? Sound familiar? Do you really believe that not talking about these things will neutralize the danger for that person? Does it really make any sense? As soon as a person gets into the realm of morality, his common sense is gone. He becomes a madman! That's why even a scientist holding a Nobel Prize in some scientific field may turn out to be a total brute in terms of moral character.

So, our whole life is but a proclamation that we believe ourselves to be our own highest good, and that our ultimate purpose is to strive for our own benefit. Simply put, the desire for happiness in the here and now is the meaning of existence for everyone born into the world. This kind of person will naturally strive to make himself feel good. But what is "good?" How do we define our *summum bonum*? I conducted a survey among believers to find out what they think about happiness in general. Here's what it boils down to: a large and comfortable home, a life-partner, a lifelong romantic relationship (for women primarily), obedient children, lots of money, good health, good work or not having to work at all, personal safety. As you may have guessed, there's no Christian worldview in this list. The list contains goals attractive for almost all of the seven billion people on the planet. But what about God? Where is He in this picture? Unfortunately, our human concept of happiness does not include God—only what we can get out of Him. This is so natural for our fallen nature.

People devote all their energy to what they believe will yield them the highest possible pleasure and bring them a fulfilling life. Remember the story about hair dryers looking for the meaning of life? They are basically looking for happiness. And what makes a hair dryer happy? The answer is simple—fulfilling the purpose for which it was made. Not a purpose that was made up, chosen, or found, but the only purpose for which it was designed, and, therefore, must embrace. The designer has already defined its purpose. Its purpose is *to do what it was made for!* Let me say it again—a product's purpose is to do what it was made for. Every man or woman is God's product; we also have a purpose, each and every one of us. We were made for a purpose. Let us explore this purpose, and, therefore, the meaning of life in general, in what follows. It's important for us to see it in the context of worship. Let me show you the connection between these two concepts.

Worship

God created human beings for *worship*. By worship I don't mean a one-time event, though it may be repeated from time to time. What we do each Sunday in church when we sing and worship together hardly demonstrates the essence and character of true worship. Worship is *a lifestyle* when you direct your efforts, creativity, time, attention, love, and adoration towards a certain goal. Worship is a value system. And the object of our worship is always our highest treasure. That's how we were designed by God. We naturally worship what we view as the most important thing in our lives. *That's what we exist for.*

    The first humans sinned when the object of their worship changed. God ceased to be their highest treasure. They started worshipping themselves. That's why sin, at its most basic level, is changing the object of worship. All sins grow out of that root. Eve reached out for the forbidden fruit precisely because of this change. Adam and Eve eventually died, just as God had warned them, although physically they endured for another nine hundred years. The spiritual state in which our forefathers ended up because of sin is called death in Scripture (Gen. 2:17). A man whose worship is not focused on God is dead! A man who doesn't have God as his highest treasure becomes so internally warped and deformed that the only fitting place for him in all eternity is the fire of hell. Just think about it.

    It was changing the object of worship that led to a change in how people viewed the meaning of life. When we define our own purpose and meaning, we usually don't consider God, not even as the last resort. But we are doomed to fail in our quest for at least two reasons. First of all, we value ourselves first and foremost. This means we cannot find any other valid reason for our existence besides our own wellbeing and happiness—by default. Secondly, we are limited in our search by the confines of this earthly life. It's useless to look for a cellphone in a room where you have never left it. No matter how hard and long you look, you cannot find something that's not there. One of the messages of the Book of Job is that God never put on any person or any other creature the all-important task of defining one's own meaning.[1] He left this task to Himself! No one in this world except God himself can give us true fulfillment. Until we become aware of it, we are doomed to scramble through the thorny byroads of this world, wasting time, falling, getting bruised, getting our feet sore and bleeding in the futile search for the true meaning.

In your mind, take a careful look at your life journey up to this moment. Most likely, by this time you own something. You probably own some property, have a spouse, children, parents, and other people whom you love or adore. You may have achieved something important, having invested a lot of time and effort into something of value. In general, you are blessed with many good things, and so *you have something to lose,* just like Job. Are you prepared, following Job's example, to elevate the worship of God as your sole purpose in life? Are you ready to worship in the midst of losses? This is what is implied in the following verses:

> "Then Job arose and tore his robe and shaved his head, and he fell to the ground and worshiped. He said, "Naked I came from my mother's womb, and naked I shall return there. The Lord gave and the Lord has taken away. Blessed be the name of the Lord." (1:20–21)

---

[1] Ecclesiastes also wrote extensively about it at a later time.

I read this on one occasion and it dawned on me that it's possible to worship God even in tears. In fact, tears are often necessary! Pain and worship are not mutually exclusive. You can howl in pain and praise the Lord in the same breath. When I first tried to do it, you wouldn't guess what I felt; I liked it! In spite of my unwillingness to praise the Lord in the midst of suffering, I forced myself to do it, and suddenly an incredible oceanic peace descended on me. I froze in utter amazement, trying to make sense out of my thoughts and sensations. God, who seemed so distant and cruel, suddenly came near and became dear. I felt comforted, though the circumstances did not change. The moment I chose to fulfill my mission—worship the Lord—my efforts were rewarded.

The main message of the book of Job is that *nothing* stands in the way of true worship. From God's point of view, worship is something entirely unconditional. Because this is our purpose in life, it follows that nothing will bring us (the new creation in us) more joy and fulfillment. Probably the most vivid expression of this joy was demonstrated by King David. He really knew what it is to worship God with self-abandonment! In my opinion, this is what singles him out from other biblical prophets. Maybe that's why the Bible calls him "a man after God's heart." He left us his Psalms, his great instructions for worship.

Satan uses the darkness in our lives to put an end to our worship. But in reality, the darkness we go through simply reveals what we worship above all else. Nothing else. That is exactly what happened in the case of Job's wife. Her sufferings revealed what she actually worshiped. God sends darkness into the lives of His children in order to enrich their worship, so they can get the second wind in their race and gain new strength. The most precious and beautiful song of praise comes from a broken heart. It is like pure gold, without any dross. "Blessed be the name of the Lord"—these words of Job are truly precious, because, from a worldly point of view, he had no valid reason to say that. Is it difficult to bless the name of the Lord when your life is comes easy? Even non-believers say things like "praise the Lord" daily—though only when their circumstances take a turn for the better, and never the other way around. And, by the way, in this case, they are using the name of the Lord in vain. But they will never say "praise the Lord" in pain, because it's impossible to praise the Lord in sufferings without faith.

Job had all the external signs of a suffering person: he tore his clothes, shaved his beard and fell prostrate. This was his way of showing that trouble had entered into his life. But it was just one side of how he perceived his situation. He worshiped the Lord and demonstrated that even such a horrendous turn of events doesn't entitle a person to clench his teeth and shake his fists against Heaven. His brief prayer echoed throughout the entire universe. The heart that was torn apart by a terrible tragedy was able to produce a cry of praise, not a curse. It came from the depths of his heart, and not without a mighty effort. Job gave glory to God, and the truth triumphed.

In order to teach humanity a lesson of "how to give with the right heart," God chose the one who was given so much more than any one of us, and then took it all away from him! It must have been done so that we would, in comparing ourselves with him, hush down our inner rebellion. Job is a fine example of how to worship God even when you have lost. Here is a man who gave away properly, because he had received properly. "Naked I came from my mother's womb, and naked I shall return there. The Lord gave and the Lord has taken away." Just feel the power of the blessing conveyed in this one sentence! First of all, we see that he knew the "rights" he had upon entering this world. He came in naked, having nothing that he could properly call his own. This is the only right attitude towards your birthrights. Second of all, he obviously knew that one day he would have to part with everything he held dear. This is the right attitude towards death. Unlike so many, he did not ignore it, but was aware of its imminence, as well as of his own poverty in drawing near to it.

Our physical death is a checkpoint between the two worlds. Its gate-keepers will strip you bare of everything you had before you are able to pass through. You will have to leave this world as naked as you came into it. All of your property, whatever you have gained here through hard work, will remain on Earth to be burned on Judgment Day. You will not be able to take anything with you, not even a button, a pin, or a crumb. All your favorite things will go to someone else: your favorite chair, your favorite mug, your favorite food, etc. You will have to part with your loved ones (those who will outlive you). Sooner or later, you will have to let go even of the hand of someone you love dearly. For someone who doesn't have faith, remembering this truth is excruciating! That's why unbelievers flee from any reminders of death. For a believer though, remembering death means to live in the real world, recognizing our full dependence on the Creator and embracing His absolute lordship. Accepting one's weaknesses and limitations is essential to true worship. Awareness of one's mortality is sanity. It encourages us to be better stewards of God's blessings in the present. For example, when I realize that death can separate me from my wife at any moment, my heart gets filled up with tenderness and appreciation of her presence now. Awareness of mortality helps me to be always ready for the transition between this world and eternity, because it can happen any moment. To deny or refuse to think about it is madness. Awareness of one's mortality helps a person not to cling to the things of this world, forgetting the fear of God. So a serious and sober attitude towards death essentially results in a serious and sober attitude towards life.

Thirdly, Job's words bear out his full acceptance of God's sovereignty. Job recognized God's right to give and to take away.

Most people will easily allow God the right to give (yes and amen!), but they will go crazy when He takes something away. Job's wife did not understand why the name of the Lord should be blessed when there were no more blessings left. She had lost her treasure, something she was living for. So naturally the meaning of life for her was lost too. Job, however, did not lose the meaning of his life because what was taken away was not the most important thing. He knew his God-given purpose, and it gave him the strength to go on, although what he experienced could hardly be called life. God was the focus of his worship, the most precious thing in his life, the One whose approval he sought above all else, and for whose glory he lived. The following words of approval from the mouth of God confirm that God was his highest treasure: ". . . a blameless and upright man, fearing God and turning away from evil" (1:8). Job's phenomenal righteousness was proceeding not from a competitive spirit but from his complete submission to God, which made all the fleshly desires dim and become unattractive. He got up in the morning, ate, talked, worked, helped others, raised children, and did everything else with just one goal in mind—*pleasing the Lord*. In doing so he was not trying to coax God into giving him more stuff, as was Satan's allegation. He did it because God was the meaning of his life. And as we can see, the Lord blessed him for his faithfulness. "The eyes of the Lord are toward the righteous and His ears are open to their cry" (Ps. 34:15).

So, the meaning of a man's life is in worshiping God (Eccl. 12:13–14). This is a certain lifestyle, when God becomes a person's highest value, and all his desires are governed by his moral law. Our highest joy is the joy of pleasing Him. When we live this way, we fulfill our purpose, and so attain to the meaning of life. We live according to God's original design, thus glorifying the Designer. Man is made in the image of God, which means we not only have privileges, but also some duties. The bearers of God's image are capable of glorifying the Creator in a more powerful and diverse way than the rest of creation, because their worship combines their moral behavior, gratitude, fellowship, creative and intellectual self-expression, and various activities. To put it simply, the galaxy, the tree-beetle, and human beings share one and the same purpose of existence—praising God. True, there is one significant difference between human beings and other creatures. Humans can disobey God and not fulfill their purpose while a bee cannot. All of creation, with the exception of man, glorifies its Creator *by just existing*. As for man, we have been dishonoring God by our existence every day. Yet, God will be glorified even through the ungodly (Prov. 16:4). In any case, the bearers of God's image are expected to do much more than just to exist. They are called to meaningful worship, which is to magnify the glory of the Almighty. Man is the only creature that robs God of His glory every single day. Those who have been given all kinds of talents and gifts live for their own self-exaltation! Having received a gift, they live as if this wonderful ability originated within themselves. They win prizes, medals, standing ovations, earn popularity and recognition, and they thank their parents, teachers, friends, spouses, children, good luck—not One to whom they owe not only their abilities, but also life itself. How insulting!

When I go to the supermarket and walk through the fruit and vegetable aisles, I usually have the following thoughts pop up in my head. First of all, I admire the abundance of God's provision heaped up on the shelves. What a variety of tastes, shapes and colors! Every time I see it, I praise God for His creativity, inventiveness and grace. He gave us the opportunity to enjoy such a plethora of tastes and smells. Some of these gifts may be unaffordable, but it doesn't prevent me from worshiping God. Next, I see people thoughtlessly shoving these gifts into their carts and bags. Here is a young mother carefully picking tomatoes. She's wrinkling her nose as she carefully examines each one and puts them in her basket. She only wants the best. Here's a middle-aged man clutching a piece of paper in his hand (probably a shopping list). He's nervously tossing whatever he lays his eyes on into his shopping cart. He goes through his list quickly and mindlessly—he just wants to get out of here as soon as possible. People are hustling and bustling all around me. "Cease striving and know that I am God; I will be exalted among the nations, I will be exalted in the earth" (Ps. 46:10). I look at these men and women with sorrow and realize that they do not need God. They do not want Him. Until the day they die, the vast majority of them will be consuming God's good gifts, taking all of His blessings for granted and even resenting Him for not giving more. I feel kind of sorry for God that He isn't getting His proper worship He is due. I am sad to see so many people running around and not even considering that they owe all this to God's kindness. Despite the ample evidence of his presence, they are overly focused on their earthly wellbeing. One part of me demands an immediate judgment on these people, but the other glorifies the Lord for His unbelievable patience towards sinners—because I am one of them! People tread on God's Earth, partake of His gifts, breathe His air. The sun rises on the wicked and the good, the rain falls on every single person, the earth grows food for those who love God and for those who hate Him. Yet, only some people will give thanks to the Lord and ascribe to him the glory due to His name.

But it will catch up with them in the end, for the end is inevitable. God's patience is enormous but not eternal. We will all die, sooner or later. Just a little longer, and the ungrateful will stand at the threshold of eternity, where they will receive an almost complete, but sadly belated revelation of the true nature of reality. They will understand with a shock how deceptive this material world is. Someone pulled a false reality over their eyes—much like in the well-known thriller "The Matrix." They will see that they have been miserable slaves of sin, having exchanged their divine glory for pig's food and having rejected with contempt the truth that could have set them free. They will see how they have wasted the precious time of their earthly journey. Everything that seemed important and appealing, everything they gave their time and energy to, will suddenly show its downside. Futility. Ashes. Emptiness. Chasing after the wind. All their lives they have been chasing after the wind. What madness! The body, your beloved body for which you cared so much, which you fed, cherished and nourished, which you gave so much of your time and effort, will be laid in the ground and eaten by worms. What a dreadful irony! An earthly king forfeits his body to the miserable and brainless worms—all the while his immortal soul is left unattended in the bondage of sin. The voice of conscience, once weak and muffled, will turn into a deafening trumpet call, which no one will ever be able to silence. The troubling thoughts about God, which used to be brushed aside as annoying gnats, will suddenly fall upon his mind in a stinging swarm, with nowhere to escape. His earthly life—the people, the work, the relationships, the connections, the entertainment, the glossy veneer of social status, the various activities of the physical world, and the body itself—all of this will be left behind, exposing the utter deformity of the soul. He will shudder when he sees his true face. He will want to hide, but where? There will be no more hiding from the scorching and piercing gaze of the One who sits enthroned in glory. He will be followed into the court of heaven by a trail of innumerable sins and abominations, which will testify against him. And there will be a voice: "For what will a man give in exchange for his soul?" (Mark 8:37). And then despair—the real, black, and bottomless despair—will break into his soul at full speed, like a hellish express, and remain there as the only sensation for the rest of eternity. All because the gentle hands of the One who was pierced and who offered himself up to redeem his soul will now wield the shining sword, exacting his wrath against all ungodliness. Damned, damned forever!

The dwelling place of those who didn't give glory to God is hell. It's a place of a total absence of God's goodness. Total! There's nothing there but wrath and fury! I don't know what exactly hell will be like, but I know it will be horrible. I suppose that all the five senses through which one enjoys God's gifts will yield nothing but suffering. Eternal darkness is reserved for the eyes (2 Pet. 2:17). Weeping and gnashing of teeth is reserved for the ears (Luke 13:28). Stench is reserved for the nose, pain for the touch, hunger for the taste. Eternal hunger and thirst are the lot of those who spat into the nourishing hand of the Creator while living in the body. There will be nothing good left, not even a single pleasant feeling out of all the myriads of possible pleasures. Nothing positive will ever be experienced again, because every good gift comes from God who was rejected. They did not even choose to say a simple "thank you" to the One who created their body and soul, who had allowed them to feel the coolness of the evening breeze, contemplate the beauty of nature, enjoy the fruits of the earth, feel the touch of someone dear, smell the aromas of the forest, relish the sound of the surf. All of this will disappear out of their lives forever, when God, in his turn, abandons them. For all eternity, there will be not a single good thing or any relief for those who rejected God as their highest good (Luke 16:24–25).

Without God, a man's life has no more meaning than that of a worm. The Lord himself is that missing element, without which our only goal of existence on earth is reproduction. But then are we any different from animals (Eccl. 3:18)? All the differences that I can think of actually make us even more guilty than we are, because, as bearers of the image of God, *we have no right* to exist without God as the ultimate reality of our lives. For the carnal mind, God is the most ignored concept. Our sin is horrendous indeed! All the various sinful acts that we engage in are but a consequence of the one primary sin—worshiping man instead of God. This is what *unbelief* is. The life an unbeliever is one continuous never-ending sin! This sin is not necessarily an act, but rather a sinful state, in which ALL thoughts, feelings, actions and words provoke God's anger (Eph. 2:1–3; Rom. 8:7–8). Each breath that this person takes is a witness against him, because he does not wish to have anything to do with the One who gives breath to all (Job 33:4).

Wisdom

As you well know, the book of Job is a book of wisdom. It is very important to understand that the wisdom exalted in the Bible is not intellectual but moral. Scripture attributes wisdom not to someone who knows much, but to someone who is trying to please the Lord. A wise man is the one who will avoid eternal punishment, for truly there is no task more important for a mortal being than this one. "The path of life leads upward for the wise that he may keep away from Sheol below" (Prov. 15:24). So, according to Scripture, a fool is not an imbecile with a stupid smirk on his face, but an *ungodly* man (Prov. 14:9, 16; 19:3). He does not care about the coming Judgment and lives without the fear of God. Indeed, only a fool will spend his short time on Earth chasing after the wind, not getting ready for the encounter with the living God. That's why all the books of wisdom convey one and the same key idea; true wisdom is the fear of God (Prov. 9:10; Eccl. 12:13–14).

The Book of Job points out the same. The entire twenty-eighth chapter is devoted to Job's reflections on wisdom. He needed it badly because he had so many questions about what was happening to him. Without wisdom, it would be impossible to have the right attitude towards his suffering. Job follows a certain logic in this chapter. Since all precious metals or precious stones have a place of origin, there must be a specific geographical location where they can be found (Job 28:1–11). So, the question is: "Where can wisdom be found? And where is the place of understanding?" (28:12). The answer—wisdom is not obtained in the same way as physical objects. It cannot be bought. There is no place on Earth where wisdom can be found, unlike precious metals and stones. No one can grant you wisdom (28:13–22). Only God knows its "location" and can reveal it to man, because He is its sole Author and Giver (28:23–27). The last verse of the chapter summarizes Job's thoughts and gives a definition of wisdom:

> "And to man He said, 'Behold, the fear of the Lord, that is wisdom; and to depart from evil is understanding." (28:28)

These words are essential to properly understand Job's godliness before and after the test. Job, his three friends, and the mysterious Elihu who came out of nowhere, were struggling with the question of why the righteous man had to suffer so much. But none of them gave an adequate explanation to what had happened. The reason is obvious. It was humanly impossible! To do so, one would have to know all mysteries and what "belongs to the Lord" (Deut. 29:29). But even if someone had witnessed the conversation between God and Satan in the courts of Heaven, he would still have not understood why God gave his precious child over to the mercy of a ferocious demon. He would only have been able to share with Job the sequence of events leading up to the tragedy. I don't think it would have been much easier for Job to endure his suffering if he was aware of being used as a racehorse on which the Lord God Himself had placed his bet. The price of winning would have been too high.

As mentioned earlier, God did not explain anything to Job or any of us who read this story in the twenty-first century. We can only see the universal and particular blessings (and we can only guess as to what some of them were) that this wager resulted in. This situation represents the reality we live in—none of us can peep behind the curtain of the ecumenical theater and read the script of the Heavenly Director in order to understand what kind of blessings will come out of the present pain. He won't give us account for His actions. In other words, when life checkmates us and gives us every sign of the inevitable defeat, the Grand Chess Master will not be in a hurry to reassure us that we, small and defenseless pawns, will one day become queens. He has already given us enough reassurance by saying that we will come out winners in the end. And we are winners, although we are not always aware of God's specific moves that lead us to victory. You will just have to trust.

Job knew that despite all his pain, all his misery, and all his losses, he would come out glorious in the end (19:25–27). As long as our hopes are fixed on the *future* glory, the fear of God will keep us from evil in the present time (Prov. 16:6). It protects us from going insane in the midst of sufferings, so we don't go as far as rejecting God and his ways. Remember Job's rebuke to his wife, "But he said to her, 'You speak as one of the foolish women speaks. Shall we indeed accept good from God and not accept adversity?' In all this Job did not sin with his lips" (Job 2:10). As you well know, this is how Job answered his wife when she suggested cursing God. In this verse, we see a classic example of how the fear of God works. Figuratively speaking, fear of God is like a safety device that helps us to survive power surges (life circumstances) without compromising our faith. It curbs our pride, which always arises from the depths of our hearts every time God allows some pain into our lives. It makes us bow down before God who appears inexplicable, alienating and distant. It gives wings to our unconditional worship. Fear of the Lord is the true wisdom, for it produces godliness even in the darkest of times. Its goal is to *keep us from evil*. In Job's case, the fear of God prevented him from crossing the line which his wife had crossed so easily. Such wisdom allows us to embrace any hardships knowing that the role of wisdom is not to necessarily explain anything, but to help us accept the situation in humility. The fear of God recognizes God's right not only to heal, but also to inflict wounds (5:18).

So, whoever has the fear of God is the true sage. Such wisdom teaches us to always focus first and foremost on pleasing the Lord. Nothing makes more sense than this high aspiration, "for what does it profit a man to gain the whole world, and forfeit his soul?" (Mark 8:36). It is a wise thing to be concerned about where you will spend all eternity, provided there are only two options. It is very wise to fear God, for He is the most powerful being in the universe (Matt. 10:28). It is wise to follow the commandments of God, because they lead to life (Deut. 32:45–47).

However, fearing God is not the same as fearing His retribution (Luke 3:7). Not wanting to be punished (which is completely natural) is not the same thing as living according to the truth. The desire to avoid the consequences of sin does not automatically translate into the right kind of fear. The wicked cannot fear the Lord, and this is their madness (Ex. 9:30). Their spiritual blindness prevents them from seeing the abomination of their own sin and the danger it entails, so they cannot properly fear God and avoid sin (Prov. 14:9). That's why whoever does not fear sin does not fear God either. The fear of God and the fear of sin go hand in hand. The fear gives us the ability to live according to the commandments of God and to please him, as all the righteous aspire to do.

This was Job's highest aspiration from his youth, and that is why he found special favor in the eyes of the Lord (Job 1:8). The name of this person was commemorated in the Bible, because there was no one like him in his days and because he remained faithful to the end. He exemplified a life lived for the glory of God, a life magnificently filled with the true meaning. Persevering to the end is well worth it if in the end you will hear God say: "Well done, good and faithful slave . . . enter into the joy of your master" (Matt. 25:21). There's *joy* for those who persevere to the end!

> *For momentary, light affliction is producing for us an*
> *eternal weight of glory far beyond all comparison,*
> *while we look not at the things which are seen,*
> *but at the things which are not seen;*
> *for the things which are seen are temporal,*
> *but the things which are not seen are eternal.*
> *(2 Cor. 4:17–18)*

Epilogue

Then all his brothers and all his sisters and all who had known him before came to him, and they ate bread with him in his house; and they consoled him and comforted him for all the adversities that the Lord had brought on him. And each one gave him one piece of money, and each a ring of gold. The Lord blessed the latter days of Job more than his beginning; and he had 14,000 sheep and 6,000 camels and 1,000 yoke of oxen and 1,000 female donkeys. He had seven sons and three daughters (42:11–13).

Being comforted is similar to receiving a compensation (Job 42:10–12; Gen. 24:67). When a person is comforted, he receives something in return for what was lost. Finally, Job was shown proper compassion by his relatives and friends. They did all they could to give him their care in compensation for what he would never get from his children. They helped him financially and, perhaps, those "golden rings and several pieces of money" became the startup capital for his future prosperity. His flocks were now double what he had before. The Lord gave him new sons and daughters in the exact the same quantity and proportion. He regained what was once lost. But as we mentioned earlier, Job was comforted even before God restored his fortunes. God Himself became Job's reward.

Wouldn't it be great if God's presence was a sufficient compensation for whatever losses we may have experienced? If it was possible for Job, then it is possible for every believer. Losses and tragedy just reveal what is in our hearts and where we draw our consolation. The hypocrite, like Job's wife, will be exposed for what he is, but the true believer will find consolation.

> "For what is the hope of the godless when he is cut off, when God requires his life? Will God hear his cry when distress comes upon him? Will he take delight in the Almighty? Will he call on God at all times?" (27:8–10)

Faith and tantrums are incompatible. For a believer, trials are never meaningless, because they come from God. Could Perfection be the cause of something pointless? Faith transforms our values and *prioritizes* them. First things become first—naturally. Sufferings loosen their grip on our lives and relinquish their gloomy power, even if they don't go away. There comes a clear understanding of the only real loss in life—the loss of God himself. The upside of Job's tragedy is that he became aware of his fear of losing God. David feared the same thing: "Do not cast me away from your presence and do not take your Holy Spirit from me" (Ps. 51:11). Everything else is vanity, futility, meaninglessness. God is the real treasure. Gaining this jewel is worth more than anything you can ever give up. When you are hurting, it's not necessary to understand why, or we wouldn't need faith. From time to time it seems necessary that we worship in darkness, where even God cannot be clearly seen.[2]

---

[2] Additionally, nothing can separate the wheat from the chaff as quickly as trials. This is also an upside of going through hard times.

Maybe you are going through some darkness in your life right now—through the endless "whys" and "what fors" which beat against the walls of your consciousness in a violent storm. There might be a hurricane of thoughts locked up in your head as in a maze of hopelessness, rushing frantically to and fro from one dead-end to another. And you don't really know how you have managed to remain sane so far. God seems silent. Your morbid mind may have already bailed out on you in this battle by destroying whatever arguments you had in favor of God's goodness. Perhaps you can feel nothing but fear and anger. But there is a way out! Don't be surprised—there is a way out! Yet it is rejected by many in their senseless pride.

I will tell you what to do in such times. WORSHIP! Worship in tears, in cries, in sobs, if nothing else works. Worship even when you feel "I don't want to" or "I can't." Forget about what you feel like. God deserves our unconditional worship. Job is an example of how to do it. He may have been wrong in some things, as we have discussed. Yet, Job's unimaginable sorrow did not fill him up with bitterness and hatred towards God who took his life as he knew it away from him." At the pinnacle of his sufferings, the Lord seemed to him a fierce and ruthless enemy (16:9–14). But despite all this, the heart of worship prevailed in his rotting body. He *chose to worship* even though he couldn't understand what was going on and did not have any answers. Receiving blow after blow from the One he loved the most and to whom he dedicated all his life, he kept blessing the hand that struck him. Not understanding why, not seeing any legitimate reasons for this tragedy, he still chose to accept the "evil" from God's hand and to suffer in a godly way. He knew what was the right thing to do, and he'd always done what was right from the days of his youth. He was guided by principles, not emotions. Let us also remember this important lesson.

I suspect that when Job first learned about the death of his children, there were some terrible words churning on his tongue, which begged to be blurted out. I suspect he was sorely tempted to say something reckless in the throes of his mental and physical agony. I suspect that he repeatedly had to deal with utter desperation. Half-dead and covered with bleeding sores, he was rescued by his strong faith, which like a mighty steed carried him out of the battlefield where he contended with the powers of hell and all their malice. There, in the pitch black darkness, without any shred of evidence for God's goodness and justice, he decided to bless the name of the Lord anyway. And you too bless His holy name. If you have faith, give glory to God and worship like Job did. This is what the Lord expects of you; do not dare to deny Him what is His own. Pull yourself together, and, if necessary, mutter thanksgiving and praises through the clenched teeth. You will see what comes out of it.

As I have already mentioned, there was a period in my life when I had to, figuratively speaking, grab myself by the scruff of the neck and worship God in spite of my feelings. I prayed in the following words:

> "Lord, the last thing I want to do now is to say 'thank you.' Gratitude and praise under such circumstances feel like mockery of common sense. My tongue sticks to the roof of my mouth, it protests against praising you. My mind implores you to answer my questions, because I cannot align the reality of my life with what I know about you. My heart is bleeding, tired of the endless pain and not wishing to entertain false hopes again. My soul's fists are clenched in sullen resolution to rebel against Heaven. My whole being is one huge 'why,' enormous like the universe itself. But my faith has not knelt under the onslaught of the heart-wrenching questions. Faith is the only thing I have left, and by this faith I give you my praise, despite all my feelings, proclaiming you as my God and Lord, to whom

belong all wisdom and perfection. You know what you are doing, and this alone is a good enough reason to humbly accept it. I *trust* in your kindness, even when I am at the end of my rope. I *trust* in your kindness and refuse to believe the lies that my eyes, ears, thoughts, and feelings tell me. My faith strengthens my hands as I hang over the abyss of despair. It is a conviction that the hardships I am going through are not meaningless, and You will save me out of trouble in your own good time. Forgive me my doubts and complaints, for I am nothing but dust."

Job knew what was right and acted accordingly. Even though we often don't always act according to the knowledge of what is right, let us remember that God never forgets those who put some effort into pleasing Him. Never! Trying to please the Lord is never pointless! (Cf. 1 Cor. 3:14.) Job humbled himself and was lifted up. "The fear of the Lord is the instruction for wisdom, and before honor comes humility" (Prov. 15:33). Job won this battle. Those who are on God's side always win, although at first it may seem otherwise. Trust my word—enduring for God's sake is worth it.

> "We count those blessed who endured. You have heard of the endurance of Job and have seen the outcome of the Lord's dealings, that the Lord is full of compassion and is merciful." (Jam. 5:11)

No price is too high when it comes to gaining God's favor. Life on earth is fleeting. God has already set the day, the hour and the minute when you will take your last breath. A little more and you, dear reader, will meet God face to face. I hope you will be happy to see each other. Remember—everything that fills you up now will immediately disappear with death. Do not grow roots on this earth; when they are torn off, it will be too painful. And one more thing—your life is but a drop in the ocean of eternity. But your eternity depends on this one drop. So even now, let God be your highest treasure. And may worshiping Him become your only purpose in life.

> *Your pride and vileness combined*
> *With lusts, and reason, and with dreams,*
> *O mortal man, your feeble mind,*
> *Oft strikes you blind, as it seems*
> *Incredible that you should fancy*
> *Yourself to be so great—in frenzy.*
> *A fleeting shadow won't stay,*
> *But turn to ashes and decay!* [3]

---

[3] Taken from "Man" by Russian poet and author A. I. Klushin (А. И. Клушин) (1763–1804), translated by Evgeny Terekhin.

www.ingramcontent.com/pod-product-compliance
Lightning Source LLC
Chambersburg PA
CBHW051359290426
44108CB00015B/2082